ADOBE® DREAMWEAVER® CS4

Dw

CLASSROOM IN A BOOK®

The official training workbook from Adobe Systems

Adobe

Adobe Press books are published by Peachpit, a division of Pearson Education located in Berkeley, California. For the latest on Adobe Press books, go to www.adobepress.com. To report errors, please send a note to errata@peachpit.com. For information on getting permission for reprints and excerpts, contact permissions@peachpit.com.

Writer: Virginia DeBolt
Project Editor: Nancy Peterson
Production Editor: Cory Borman
Development Editor: Bob Lindstrom
Technical Editors: Jim Maivald, Judith Stern
Copyeditors: Elissa Rabellino, Dan Foster
Compositor: Owen Wolfson
Indexer: Karin Arrigoni
Media Producer: Eric Geoffroy
Cover Design: Eddie Yuen
Interior Design: Mimi Heft

Printed and bound in the United States of America
ISBN-13:   978-0-321-57381-0
ISBN-10:   0-321-57381-1

9 8 7 6 5 4 3 2 1

WHAT'S ON THE DISC

Here is an overview of the contents of the Classroom in a Book disc

Lesson files ... and so much more

The *Adobe Dreamweaver CS4 Classroom in a Book* disc includes the lesson files that you'll need to complete the exercises in this book, as well as other content to help you learn more about Adobe Dreamweaver CS4 and use it with greater efficiency and ease. The diagram below represents the contents of the disc, which should help you locate the files you need.

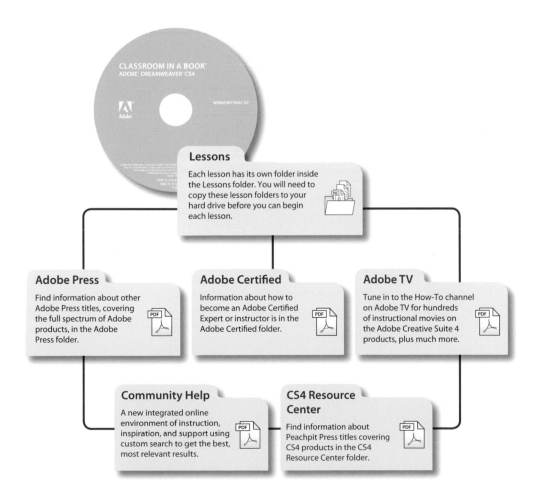

Lessons

Each lesson has its own folder inside the Lessons folder. You will need to copy these lesson folders to your hard drive before you can begin each lesson.

Adobe Press

Find information about other Adobe Press titles, covering the full spectrum of Adobe products, in the Adobe Press folder.

Adobe Certified

Information about how to become an Adobe Certified Expert or instructor is in the Adobe Certified folder.

Adobe TV

Tune in to the How-To channel on Adobe TV for hundreds of instructional movies on the Adobe Creative Suite 4 products, plus much more.

Community Help

A new integrated online environment of instruction, inspiration, and support using custom search to get the best, most relevant results.

CS4 Resource Center

Find information about Peachpit Press titles covering CS4 products in the CS4 Resource Center folder.

CONTENTS

GETTING STARTED

Adobe® Dreamweaver® CS4 is the industry-leading web authoring program. Whether you create websites for a living or plan to create one for your own business, Dreamweaver offers all the tools you need to get professional-quality results.

About *Classroom in a Book*

Adobe Dreamweaver CS4 Classroom in a Book® is part of the official training series for graphics and publishing software from Adobe Systems, Inc.

The lessons are designed so that you can learn at your own pace. If you're new to Dreamweaver, you'll learn the fundamentals of putting the program to work. If you are an experienced user, you'll find that *Classroom in a Book* teaches many advanced features, including tips and techniques for using the latest version of Dreamweaver.

Although each lesson includes step-by-step instructions for creating a specific project, you'll have room for exploration and experimentation. You can follow the book from start to finish, or complete only those lessons that correspond to your interests and needs. Each lesson concludes with a Review section containing questions and answers on the subjects you've covered.

Prerequisites

Before using *Adobe Dreamweaver CS4 Classroom in a Book*, you should have a working knowledge of your computer and its operating system. Be sure you know how to use the mouse, standard menus, and commands, and also how to open, save, and close files. If you need to review these techniques, see the printed or online documentation that was included with your Microsoft Windows or Apple Macintosh operating system.

● **Note:** When instructions differ by platform, Windows commands appear first, followed by the Mac OS command—for example, "Press Alt (Windows) or Option (Mac) and click outside the graphic."

Installing the program

Before you perform any exercises in this book, verify that your computer system meets the hardware requirements for Dreamweaver, that it's correctly configured, and that all required software is installed.

You must purchase the Adobe Dreamweaver CS4 software separately. For complete instructions on installing the software, see the "How to Install" file on the Adobe Dreamweaver CD.

Copying the *Classroom in a Book* files

The *Classroom in a Book* CD includes folders containing all the files necessary for the lessons. Each lesson has its own folder. You must install these folders on your hard disk to perform the exercises in each lesson. To conserve space on your hard disk, you can individually install a folder for each lesson as you need it. It is vitally important that you store all lesson folders within a single folder on your hard drive. This master folder will serve as the local root site folder, as described in Lesson 2.

To install the *Classroom in a Book* files:

1 Insert the *Adobe Dreamweaver CS4 Classroom in a Book* CD into your computer's optical disc drive.

2 Create a folder on your hard disk. Name the folder "DW CIB." This will be the local site root folder.

3 Do one of the following:

- Copy all the contents of the Lessons folder into the newly created folder.

- Copy only the single lesson folder you currently need into the newly created folder.

In addition, you must copy four additional folders to the DW CIB folder on your hard drive: SpryAssets, images, movie, and Scripts. These folders are used in several lessons and must remain in your DW CIB folder.

Setting preferences

To perform the exercises in these lessons, make sure your preferences are set correctly.

1 Open Adobe Dreamweaver CS4.

2 Choose Edit > Preferences (Windows) or Dreamweaver > Preferences (Mac).

3   In the Preferences dialog box, in the Category list, click Accessibility.

4 Select all four check boxes in the "Show attributes when inserting" area.

5 Click OK.

Setting up the workspace

Dreamweaver includes a number of workspaces to accommodate various computer configurations and individual workflows. For this book, the best workspace to use is the Classic setup.

1 In Dreamweaver CS4, locate the Application Bar. If necessary, choose Window > Application Bar to display it.

2 The default workspace is called Designer. Use the pop-up menu to choose other workspaces, such as Coder, Classic, and Designer Compact. In some workspace setups, the Insert menu is displayed in a large panel; in others, the Insert menu is in a more compact bar.

3 Choose Classic when performing the exercises in this book. Most of the book's workspace images use the Classic setup with the Insert menu in a bar. When you finish the lessons in this book, experiment using various workspaces to find the one that you prefer.

4 Choose Window > Application Bar to hide the Application Bar.

Finding Dreamweaver information

For complete, up-to-date information about Dreamweaver panels, tools, and other application features, visit the Adobe website. Choose Help > Dreamweaver Help. You'll be connected to the Adobe Community Help website where you can search Dreamweaver Help and support documents, and locate other websites relevant to Dreamweaver users. You can also narrow your search results to view only Adobe Help and support documents.

If you plan to use Dreamweaver when you're not connected to the Internet, you can download the current PDF version of Dreamweaver Help at www.adobe.com/go/documentation.

For additional information resources, such as tips, techniques, and the latest product information, visit the Adobe Community Help page at community.adobe.com/help/main.

● Note: If Dreamweaver detects that you are not connected to the Internet when you open the application, choose Help > Dreamweaver Help to open the Help HTML pages that are installed with Dreamweaver. For more up-to-date information, view the online Help files or download the current Dreamweaver Help PDF.

Checking for updates

Adobe periodically provides software updates. You can obtain these updates using Adobe Updater, if you have an active Internet connection.

1   In Dreamweaver, choose Help > Updates. The Adobe Updater automatically checks for updates for your Adobe software.

2   In the Adobe Updater dialog box, select the updates you want to install, and then click Download And Install Updates to install them.

⬤ **Note: To choose preferences for future updates, click Preferences. You can choose how often Adobe Updater should check for updates, identify applications to be updated, and whether to download them automatically. Click OK to accept the new settings.**

Additional resources

Adobe Dreamweaver CS4 Classroom in a Book is not meant to replace the documentation that comes with the program, nor is it a comprehensive reference for every feature in Dreamweaver CS4. Only the commands and options used in these lessons are explained in this book. For comprehensive information about program features, refer to these resources:

• Adobe Dreamweaver CS4 Community Help, which you can view by choosing Help > Dreamweaver Help. Community Help is an integrated online environment of instruction, inspiration, and support. It includes custom searching of expert-selected, relevant content in Adobe.com and other sites. Community Help combines content from Adobe Help, Support, Design Center, Developer Connection, and Forums—along with great online community content that help users find the best and most up-to-date resources. You can access tutorials, technical support, online product help, videos, articles, tips and techniques, blogs, examples, and much more.

• Adobe Dreamweaver CS4 Support Center, where you can find and browse the support and learning content on Adobe.com. Visit www.adobe.com/support/dreamweaver/.

• Adobe TV, where you will find programming on Adobe products, including a channel for professional photographers and a How To channel that contains hundreds of movies on Dreamweaver CS4 and other products across the Adobe Creative Suite 4 lineup. Visit http://tv.adobe.com/.

Also check out these useful links:

• The Dreamweaver CS4 product home page at www.adobe.com/products/dreamweaver/.

- Dreamweaver user forums at www.adobe.com/support/forums/ for peer-to-peer discussions of Adobe products.

- Dreamweaver Exchange at www.adobe.com/cfusion/exchange/ for extensions, functions, code, and more.

- Dreamweaver plug-ins at www.adobe.com/products/plugins/dreamweaver/.

Adobe certification

The Adobe Certified program is designed to help Adobe customers and trainers improve and promote their product proficiency skills. Four levels of certification are offered:

- Adobe Certified Associate (ACA)

- Adobe Certified Expert (ACE)

- Adobe Certified Instructor (ACI)

- Adobe Authorized Training Center (AATC)

The Adobe Certified Associate (ACA) credential certifies that individuals have the entry level skills to plan, design, build, and maintain effective communications using various forms of digital media.

The Adobe Certified Expert program is a way for expert users to upgrade their credentials. You can use Adobe certification as a catalyst for getting a raise, finding a job, or promoting your expertise.

If you are an ACE-level instructor, the Adobe Certified Instructor program takes your skills to the next level and gives you access to a wide range of Adobe resources.

Adobe Authorized Training Centers offer instructor-led courses and training on Adobe products, employing only Adobe Certified Instructors. A directory of AATCs is available at http://partners.adobe.com.

For information on the Adobe Certified program, visit www.adobe.com/support/certification/main.html.

1 GETTING A QUICK START

In this lesson, you'll be introduced to Dreamweaver while building a sample web page and learning how to work within the Dreamweaver workspace. You'll learn how to do the following:

- Define a site in Dreamweaver
- Explore the Dreamweaver workspace
- Create a new page using a CSS (Cascading Style Sheets) Layout
- Save a document
- Modify the page title and change text headings
- Insert text from an external document
- Add foreground and background images
- Create, modify, and select CSS styles
- Work with Code view and Code and Design view
- Preview your page in Live view or a browser

 This lesson will take about 60 minutes to complete. Before beginning, be sure you have copied the Lessons > lesson01 folder and the images folder from the *Adobe Dreamweaver CS4 Classroom in a Book* CD to your hard drive.

See Umbria with us

You have the fun. We do the work.

Come enjoy the vacation of a lifetime! We do the work and you have the fun! Our tour through the hill towns of Umbria is unequalled. *For two weeks, you'll enjoy worry-free pampering.*

Every day, a delicious breakfast and dinner (with wine) are included. Lunch is on your own. Travel in air conditioned buses on ten wonderful day trips to the surrounding beautiful, historic hill towns.

Our luxury hotel accommodations include a hot tub, pool, and nearby by night time entertainment. Your weekend is free to schedule as you wish, but your meals are always provided by our excellent chefs.

Umbria Hill Town Tours, Terni, Italy
Contact Us

Use Dreamweaver's expertly designed CSS layouts to quickly create a standards-based page, ready for your personalized content.

Defining a Dreamweaver site

The lessons in this book function within a Dreamweaver site. In Dreamweaver, you work with a local site stored in a folder on your hard drive. When you are ready to publish your site (see Lesson 11, "Publishing to the Web"), you also work with a remote site, stored on your web host's computer. The folder structures and files of the two sites are essentially mirrors of each other.

First, set up your local site.

1 Open Adobe Dreamweaver CS4. If you have not previously opened Dreamweaver CS4, you'll want to fill in the registration screen.

2 Choose Site > New Site and the Site Definition for DW CIB dialog box appears. If the Advanced view isn't selected, click Advanced.

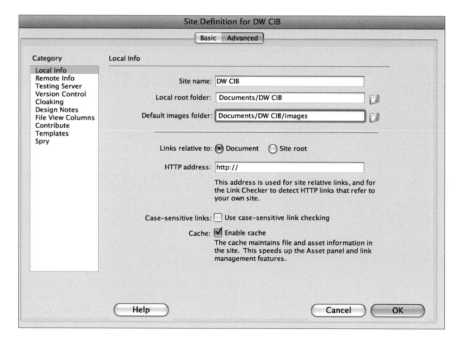

The Basic view of the Site Definition dialog box, while less technical, does require that you enter more preliminary information. By choosing the Advanced view, you need to set only a part of the site definition to get started.

3 Choose the Local Info category of the Site Definition dialog box, if necessary. In the Site name field, type **DW CIB**, and press Tab.

Site names are listed in the Files panel and are typically related to a specific project or client.

4 Next to the "Local root folder" field, click the folder icon. When the "Choose local root folder for site DW CIB" dialog box opens, navigate to the DW CIB

folder containing the files that you copied from the *Adobe Dreamweaver CS4 Classroom in a Book* CD and click Select (Windows) or Choose (Mac).

5 Next to the "Default images folder" field, click the folder icon. When the dialog box opens, navigate to the DW CIB/images folder containing the files you copied from the Dreamweaver CS4 Classroom in a Book CD and click Select (Windows) or Choose (Mac).

6 In the Site Definition dialog box, click OK to confirm your choices.

Now that you've set up your site, you can easily open files within Dreamweaver. Defining a site is a crucial first step in beginning any project in Dreamweaver. Knowing where the site root folder is located determines link pathways and enables many site-wide options in Dreamweaver such as site-wide Find and Replace.

Using the Welcome screen

The Welcome screen provides quick access to recent pages, easy creation of a range of page types, and a direct connection to several key help topics. The Welcome screen appears when you first start the program or when no other documents are open. Let's use the Welcome screen to explore ways to open a document.

1 In the Create New column of the Welcome screen, click HTML to open a new, blank page.

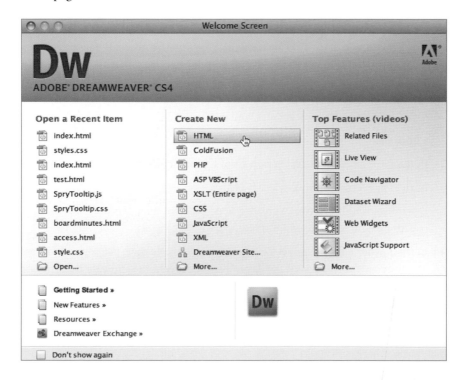

2 Choose File > Close.

If any changes were made, the file should be saved.

3 Return to the Welcome screen and click the Open button. This allows you browse for files to open in Dreamweaver. Click Cancel.

The Welcome screen shows you a list of recently used files. Recently used files are shown in the figure above; however, your installation may not display any used files at this point. Choosing a file from this list is a quick alternative to choosing File > Open when you want to edit an existing page.

You will use the Welcome screen several times in this book. When you've completed the lessons in this book, you may prefer not to use the Welcome screen. If so, you can disable it by selecting the "Don't show again" option in the lower left of the window. You can re-enable the Welcome screen in the General category of Preferences. You can open a new page using the File menu.

Selecting a CSS layout

Adobe Dreamweaver CS4 provides 32 CSS layout files, all with different designs. In this exercise, you'll select one and modify it. The CSS layouts are carefully tested to comply with web standards and to work cross-platform on all major browsers with no additional changes to the layout. Popular two- and three-column choices are included, as well as choices that are fixed width (shown with a lock symbol); percentage- or em-based (shown with a spring symbol to indicate elasticity); and with mixtures of pixels, percentages, and ems.

1 Choose File > New.

2 In the New Document dialog box, from the first column, choose Blank Page.

3 In the Page Type column, select HTML.

Dreamweaver allows you to create a wide range of page types. HTML is the page type commonly used for building basic web pages.

4 In the Layout column, select "2 column fixed, left sidebar, header and footer." The preview for this layout displays a padlock symbol to indicate that the width is fixed at a set number of pixels. Other layouts display a spring symbol to indicate that the width will expand or contract with the browser window.

5 Leave all other options at their default settings, and click Create.

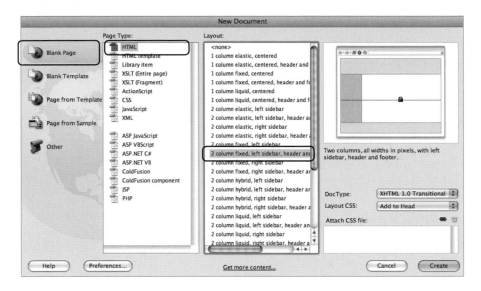

Your new page appears in Dreamweaver as a document with filler text. This is the Document window where you add your own content and customize the appearance of the page.

Saving a page

After you've created a page, it's a good idea to save it right away.

1   Choose File > Save. Alternatively, you could press Control+S (Windows) or Command+S (Mac).

2   When the Save As dialog box appears, navigate to the lesson01 folder. In the filename field, type **umbria.htm** or **umbria.html**. It's a matter of personal preference whether you use *.htm* or *.html* as your file extension. Just remember to be consistent. (This book will use *.html*.) Most websites use the filename index.html for the home page. In Lesson 9, you'll build a home page for the practice site you will create in the course of compositing the lessons in the book.

3   Click Save.

Choosing a document view

Although you'll do most web authoring in Dreamweaver in the Design window, the Document window offers you four different views:

- Design view—Renders a page in a browser-like context.

- Code view—Displays a page's source code.

- Code and Design view—Combines both Design and Code views. Click the Split button to display this view.

- Live view—Renders a page in a live browser within Dreamweaver.

The Design, Code, and Code and Design (Split) views are tightly connected. Any changes made in one become instantly viewable in the others. You will work with each view later in this lesson.

Modifying the page title

The title of a web page is displayed in the browser's title bar. Page titles are one of the key elements used by search engines to index websites. It's important to always change Dreamweaver's default page title of "Untitled Document" to a phrase that describes your specific web page.

1 If necessary, click the Design button to view the page in Design view.

2 In the Title field of the Document toolbar, select the placeholder text, *Untitled Document*.

3 Type **Umbria Hill Town Tours** and press Enter (Windows) or Return (Mac).

Changing headings

Placeholder headings are easily modified in Dreamweaver. Placeholder headings and text help you visualize the layout as it will appear when your final content is placed on the page. Changing the placeholder text is a simple process.

1 Double-click the placeholder text, *Header*, to select it. Then type **See Umbria with us**.

Dreamweaver provides a number of methods for selecting text that operate similar to word processing software—such as double-clicking a single word or dragging the mouse to highlight text. You can triple-click to select an entire paragraph.

2   Place your mouse pointer in front of the placeholder text, Main Content, and drag the pointer across the phrase to select it.

3   With the text selected, type **You have the fun. We do the work**.

You replaced the text, but the <h1> format of the text remains.

4   Choose File > Save.

Tip: You can drag the mouse pointer to select any range of text in Dreamweaver.

Inserting text

You can change paragraph text as easily as you changed the heading text. While you can enter text manually, Dreamweaver provides a robust engine for inserting text copied from other sources, such as Microsoft Office, while retaining as much of the formatting as you desire.

1   Place your mouse pointer in front of the placeholder paragraph text and drag to the end of the text so that the second placeholder heading and all paragraphs are selected. Be careful not to select "Footer."

2   Press Delete to remove the selection.

3   In Windows Explorer (Windows) or the Finder (Mac), navigate to the CD files that you copied to your hard drive and open lesson01 > vacation.rtf.

4   When the file opens, select all the text and press Control+C (Windows) or Command+C (Mac) to copy the text to the Clipboard.

5 In Dreamweaver, position the mouse pointer below the header, *You have the fun. We do the work.* Press Control+V (Windows) or Command+V (Mac) to paste the text from the Clipboard.

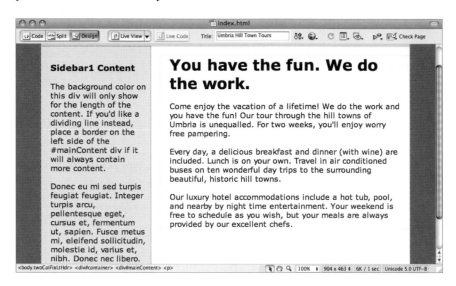

The text is automatically formatted as paragraphs <p>.

6 Place the pointer in the footer area. Select the placeholder text, "Footer." Type **Umbria Hill Town Tours**.

7 Create a line break by pressing Shift+Enter (Windows) or Shift+Return (Mac). Then, type **Contact Us**.

Umbria Hill Town Tours
Contact Us|

Inserting images

Inserting images and graphics in Dreamweaver is very straightforward. Once an image has been placed on a page, its image properties, such as alignment, can be adjusted using the Properties panel or within CSS.

1 Select all the content in the sidebar, including the placeholder header Sidebar1 Content and the two subsequent paragraphs.

2 Press Delete to remove the placeholder text.

3 In the tag selector, located at the bottom of the Document window, click <h3> and press Delete to remove the <h3> tag.

4 If the Insert panel is not visible, display it by selecting Window > Insert. It will appear as a panel. (You'll later learn how to make the panel appear in the classic workspace arrangement as a compact bar.) In the Common category of the Insert panel, click the Images menu button and choose Image.

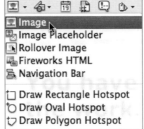

5 In the Select Image Source dialog box, navigate to the files that you copied to your hard drive and choose images > sculpted-garden.jpg. Click OK (Windows) or Choose (Mac) to confirm your choice.

6 In the Image Tag Accessibility Attributes dialog box, type **sculpted garden** in the "Alternate text" field. Click OK.

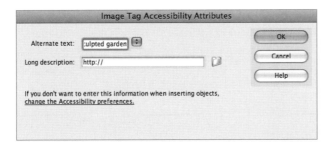

It is a good practice to enter a brief alternate description of images that add content to your page. The Alternate Text, or alt text, is seen when the image is not visible. Users with certain mobile devices, screen readers, or other browsing devices may not see images. The Alternate Text will appear for them and help them understand the content of the page. A long description is needed only when describing complex images such as charts.

See Umbria with us

You have the fun. We do the work.

Come enjoy the vacation of a lifetime! We do the work and you have the fun! Our tour through the hill towns of Umbria is unequalled. For two weeks, you'll enjoy worry free pampering.

Every day, a delicious breakfast and dinner (with wine) are included. Lunch is on your own. Travel in air conditioned buses on ten wonderful day trips to the surrounding beautiful, historic hill towns.

Our luxury hotel accommodations include a hot tub, pool, and nearby by night time entertainment. Your weekend is

7 Place your mouse pointer at the start of the main content paragraph that starts with the words *Come enjoy*, and choose Images in the Insert panel.

8 In the Select Image Source dialog box, select images > italian-hill-town.jpg and click OK (Windows) or Choose (Mac).

9 Type **Italian hill town** as the alternate text. Click OK.

10 If the Properties panel is not visible, choose Window > Properties.

11 With the newly inserted image selected, choose fltrt from the Class pop-up menu in the Properties panel.

The class fltrt (an abbreviation of *float right*) is a CSS style that will float the image to the right. Text will flow around the image.

The class fltlft (an abbreviation for *float left*) would float the image to the left with text wrapping around it on the right. All 32 CSS starting layouts have .fltrt and .fltlft in their included styles.

The float property moves an element to the right or the left of its container. (In this exercise, the container is mainContent.) When an element floats, other content flows or wraps around it. When an element floats to the right, it moves to the right and other content wraps around it on the left.

See Umbria with us

You have the fun. We do the work.

Come enjoy the vacation of a lifetime! We do the work and you have the fun! Our tour through the hill towns of Umbria is unequalled. For two weeks, you'll enjoy worry free pampering.

Every day, a delicious breakfast and dinner (with wine) are included. Lunch is on your own. Travel in air conditioned buses on ten wonderful day trips to the surrounding beautiful, historic hill towns.

Our luxury hotel accommodations include a hot tub, pool,

The page now contains both text and images. By choosing a CSS layout, modifying the text, and adding images, you have produced a web page that looks good and would work cross-browser if it were uploaded to the Internet. In the next exercise, you will improve on the appearance by modifying the CSS styles.

12 Choose File > Save.

Selecting and modifying CSS styles

Modern web pages use Cascading Style Sheets (CSS) for styling and layout. A web page is often compared to a three-legged stool, held up by the HTML, the CSS, and the JavaScript that goes into its construction. HTML is the content—the material you enter in the Design view window. CSS is the appearance and the layout—where elements are, the colors, and the backgrounds. JavaScript adds interactive function.

In this exercise, you'll modify the background color of the existing page, add a background graphic to a page section, and adjust several text attributes. All of these changes are accomplished using Dreamweaver's CSS Styles panel.

Changing the page body background color

CSS can be used to alter the style properties of any HTML tag, such as the <body> tag.

1 Choose Window > CSS Styles.

The CSS Styles panel opens.

2 In the CSS Styles panel, click All to switch from Current mode, if necessary.

All mode displays all the CSS styles associated with the current page. You must have a document open in the document window to see any styles in the CSS Styles panel.

3 Expand the <style> entry in the All Rules pane by clicking the Plus (+) button (Windows) or the expander arrow (Mac).

In lesson01, the style rules are in the document head. Dreamweaver indicates that the styles are internal to the document with brackets: <style>. In later lessons you will work with styles stored in an external style sheet. Dreamweaver will list these style sheets by name (for example, mystyles.css) in the CSS styles panel.

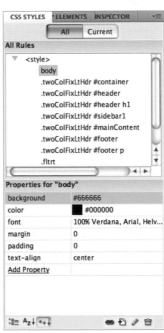

4 Select body and click Edit Rule, the pencil icon at the bottom of the CSS Styles panel.

5 When the CSS Rule definition for "body" dialog box appears, select the Background category. Click the Background color box to open the color picker.

6 In the color picker, use the eyedropper to click the white color block.

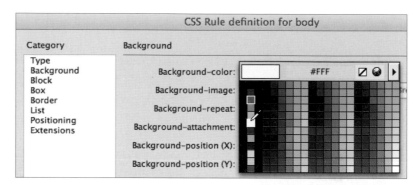

Dreamweaver automatically inserts the hexadecimal value for white, #FFF, in the Background-color field.

7 Click OK to complete the change.

Dreamweaver notes the new color in the Properties pane of the CSS Styles panel. You may have to drag down the bottom border of the CSS Styles panel to enlarge the Properties pane to see the color.

8 For a full screen view, press F4 to hide all panels.

Note that the body background color has now changed from gray to white. The header, sidebar, and footer background colors have not changed.

9 Press F4 again to restore the panels. Docked panels can be hidden and shown by pressing the F4 key or choosing Window > Hide/Show Panels. Reveal the hidden panels from the edge by positioning the mouse pointer over the reveal strips (dark gray bars shown at the edges of the application where the docked panels were located originally.) When you move the mouse pointer away from the panels, they hide again until you press F4.

Like the <body> element, other elements on the page—for example, <div#sidebar1> —can be assigned individual background-color values. To change any element's background-color value, select it in the tag selector and click the Edit Rule icon to make changes.

10 Choose File > Save.

Inserting a graphic background into the header

While foreground images are inserted directly onto the page, background images are placed using CSS.

1 Place your mouse pointer anywhere in the header text, *See Umbria with us*.

2 From the tag selector, choose <div#header>.

This selection indicates the <div> tag with an ID of #header. Note that the selected header div is outlined with a blue line in the Document window when the element is selected using the tag selector.

<body.twoColFixLtHdr> <div#container> <div#header> <h1>   ▸ ✍ ☌ Q   100% ⬧   873 x 271 ⬧   78K / 12 sec   Unicode 5.0 UTF-8

3   In the CSS Styles panel, click Current to switch to Current mode.

4   If necessary, change the About pane to Rules by clicking the "Show cascade of rules for selected tag" icon. In the Rules pane, select .twoColFixLtHdr #header h1. You may need to enlarge the CSS Styles panel to see everything properly.

5   When the "CSS Rule definition for .twoColFixLtHdr #header" dialog box appears, select the Background category. Click the Browse button next to the Background-image field.

The Select Image Source dialog box appears.

6   In the Select Image Source dialog box, navigate to images/cloud_header.jpg. Click Choose.

7   From the Background-repeat pop-up menu, choose no-repeat. Click OK.

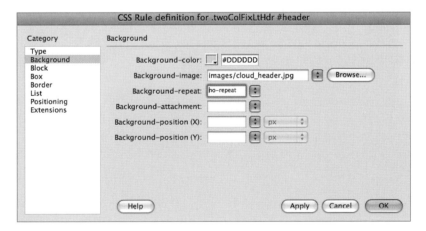

8   Click anywhere on the page to deselect the header, and view the background image.

The black header text is a bit difficult to read against the sky-blue background. So, you'll adjust the header text color in the next exercise.

Adjusting text, fonts, and colors

CSS gives you tremendous control over page appearance. In addition to changing the look and feel of all the instances of a tag on a page—or in an entire site—you can also target a style change to affect a tag in a specific location.

1   Place your mouse pointer anywhere in the header text, *See Umbria with us*.

2   From the tag selector, choose <h1>.

3 In the CSS Styles panel, select Current mode. (If All mode is selected, click Current.)

4 In the Rules pane, click Show cascade of rules for selected tag 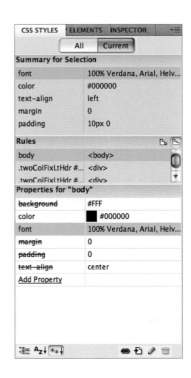. Select .twoColFixLtHdr #header h1 from the Cascade.

5 Click Edit Rule.

6 When the "CSS Rule definition for .twoColFixLtHdr #header h1" dialog box appears, from the Category column choose Type.

7 From the Font-family list, choose different fonts, such as Georgia, "Times New Roman", Times, serif, or other fonts available on your list.

Not all computers have the same fonts installed, so font choices are usually given in groups. The first group listed is your first choice, the second is your second choice, and so on. Most font choice lists usually end in either serif or sans-serif, so that if none of your choices are available, the font will at least be an available, serif or sans-serif option. Notice the Edit Font List option, which allows you to create new groups of font choices.

8 Click the color box to open the pop-up color picker, and use the eyedropper to select white. Click OK to confirm your changes.

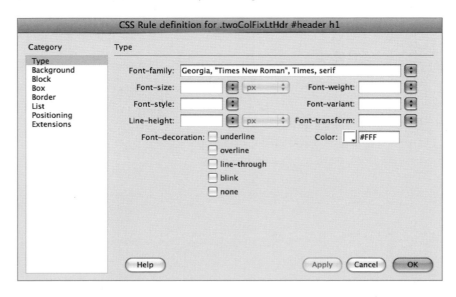

9 Click anywhere on the page to deselect the header text.

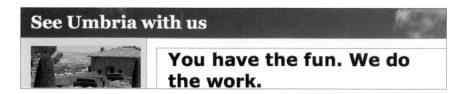

You have successfully changed both the font-family and color of the <h1> text. Other text elements on the page could be given new font-family or color values in the same manner.

Altering text size

In addition to changing the font style and color, as in the previous exercise, you can also alter text size with CSS.

1 Place your mouse pointer anywhere in the main content heading or paragraph.

2 From the tag selector, choose <div#mainContent>.

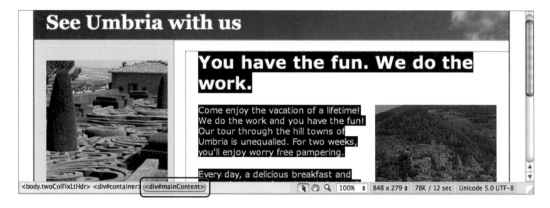

3 Click the All button. With .twoColFixLtHdr #mainContent selected in the All Rules pane of the CSS Styles panel, click Edit Rule.

4 When the "CSS Rule definition for .twoColFixLtHdr #mainContent" dialog box appears, from the Category column choose Type.

5 The font size is set to 100% for this CSS layout in the body rule. To change the font size for the mainContent div, in the Font-size field type **90**, and choose % from the options menu just to the right of the font-size field. Click OK.

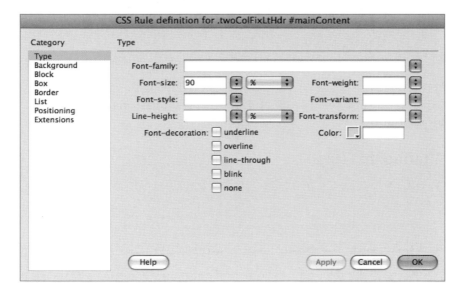

The font is now slightly smaller for all text in the mainContent div. Although it was fine at 100%, this small change demonstrates the way that any font size can be changed in Dreamweaver.

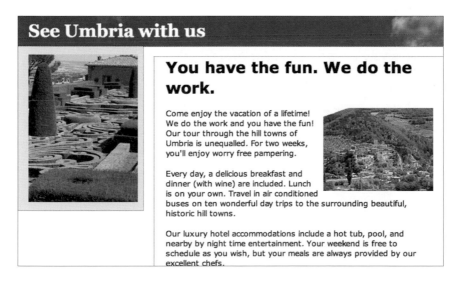

6 Choose File > Save.

Working with Code view and Code and Design view

1 If you closed umbria.html after the last exercise, in the Open a Recent Item area of the Welcome screen, click lesson01 > umbria.html.

2 In first paragraph, select the phrase *We do the work and you have the fun!*

3 In the Document toolbar, located directly above the Document window, click the Code button 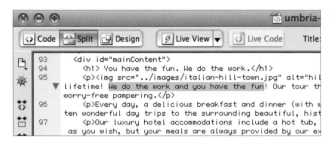.

Any selections in the document you make are also selected in Code view. A change in one view makes the same change in the other view.

Sometimes it's helpful to see the Design view and the source code simultaneously. Code and Design view allows you to do that.

4 In the Document toolbar, click the Split button ![Split] to see how the Code and Design views work together.

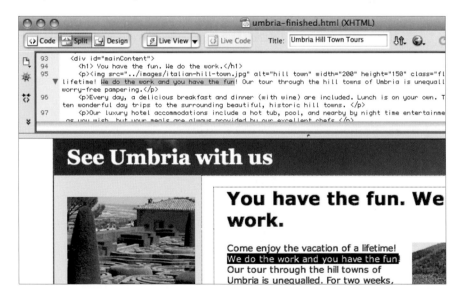

5 Position your mouse pointer on the border between the source code and the Design view until you see the horizontal border cursor ⬍. Drag the border so that the two views use equal amounts of screen space.

6 If necessary, in Design view, reselect the sentence *We do the work and you have the fun!* Type **You have the fun and we do the work!** Note that your edit is instantly visible in both views.

7 In the Code view section of the Document window, locate the words *worry free*. Delete the space between the two words; then type a hyphen (-) to change the words to *worry-free*. Note that the Design view is not updated yet.

8 Click anywhere in the Design view to confirm your code changes and update the page.

● **Note:** When you're working in the Code view, Dreamweaver waits to make sure you've completed your modifications before refreshing the Design view. You can signal that you're done making changes by clicking in the Design view or by choosing Refresh Design View ↻ in the Document toolbar.

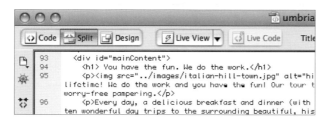

Working with horizontally- and vertically-split views

When working in Code and Design view, you may choose either a horizontally- or vertically-split view.

1 Choose View > Split Vertically.

The vertically-split Code and Design view functions exactly like the horizontally-split view. Changes in one view are automatically reflected in the other.

The Code and Design view goes one step farther, however, and gives you some useful options for working in Code and Design view with the code.

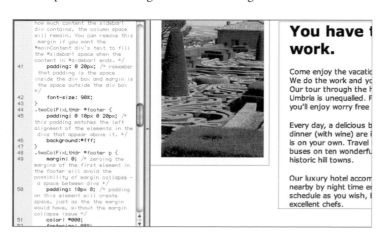

2 In the Document toolbar, click the Code button 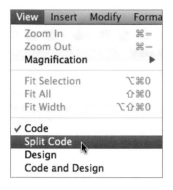.

3 Choose View > Split Code.

Two views of the page code are displayed side by side. You can scroll independently through the code in both sections. You can copy and paste from one section of the page to another using Split Code view. All changes in one section of Split Code are applied in the other Split Code section.

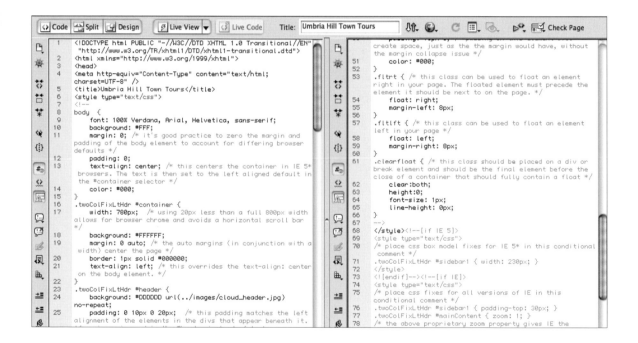

4 To view the code split horizontally, deselect View > Split Vertically.

The view changes to a horizontal arrangement.

Actions in Split Code view such as editing code are applied in both windows, and will appear when you switch back to Design view.

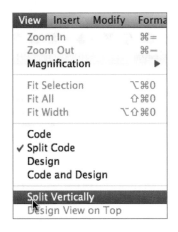

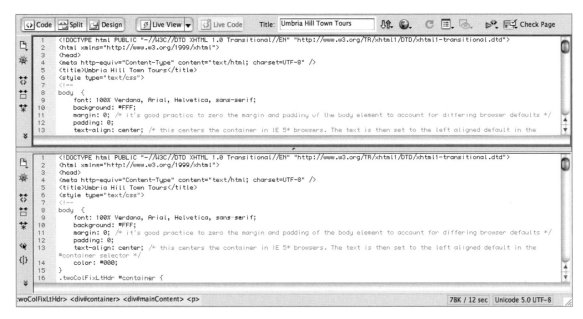

5 In the Document toolbar, click the Design button.

6 Choose File > Save. Leave the current file open for your work in the next section if you are continuing the lesson; otherwise, click File > Close.

Using the Properties panel

Note: The Properties panel uses the B and I buttons as shorthand for the old-style boldface and italics text. The actual tags are **<strong>** for B and **<em>** (an abbreviation for emphasis) for I. Some browsers render **<strong>** as bold, and **<em>** as italics, but not all do so. It's good practice to create CSS rules for both **<strong>** and **<em>** so they appear as you want.

Although Dreamweaver's Properties panel is, essentially, just another panel, it deserves special mention for its flexibility and its central role in a web designer's workflow. The options in the Properties panel change according to the current selection. For example, when text is selected, the text Properties panel appears with tools available for applying formats and adjusting text alignment. If an image is selected, the image Properties panel displays the height and width values of the image, as well as links to image-editing tools such as Adobe Photoshop or Adobe Fireworks. In this exercise, you'll open the Properties panel and use some of its most common interface elements.

1   If necessary, open File > Open Recent > umbria.html.

2   If you don't see the Properties panel under the Document window, choose Window > Properties.

3   In the tag selector at the bottom of the Document window, select `<body.twoColFixLtHdr>`.

The Properties panel window is divided into two views: HTML and CSS. The properties displayed depend upon whether the HTML or the CSS button is selected. Other controls in the Properties panel, such as the Bold and Italic buttons, are toggles: Click once to select and again to deselect. An enabled toggle appears recessed as if the button has been pushed in.

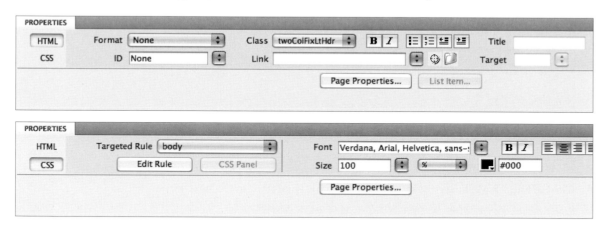

4   Click the HTML button.

5   In the Document window, select the sentence *For two weeks, you'll enjoy worry-free pampering.*

6 Click the I button to change the text to emphasized text.

> Come enjoy the vacation of a lifetime!
> We do the work and you have the fun!
> Our tour through the hill towns of
> Umbria is unequalled. *For two weeks,*
> *you'll enjoy worry-free pampering.*

7 In the Properties panel, click the CSS button.

8 In the tag selector, select <em>.

9 From the Targeted Rule menu, choose <New CSS Rule>.

10 In the Properties panel, click Edit Rule.

The New CSS Rule dialog box opens.

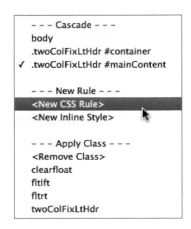

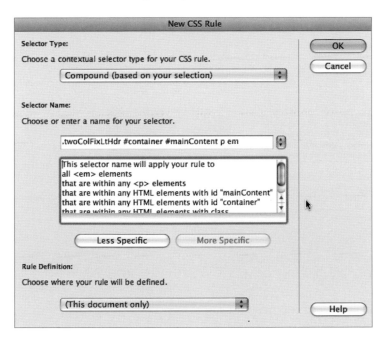

For Selector Name, Dreamweaver suggests a name based on your selection. It explains what that selector name will apply to.

11 Click Less Specific until the Selector Name field reads *#mainContent p em*.

12 Click OK.

The "CSS Rule definition for #mainContent p em" dialog box opens.

● **Note:** The CSS layouts all use a class applied to the body element. In this layout, the body is assigned to the class .twoColFixLtHdr. If you plan to use a combination of layouts—such as a three-column home page and two-column inner pages—then you would need to keep the more specific selector name. For the exercises in this book, a less specific selector will do.

13 Use the color picker to select a new color—any value other than white (such as the #00F value shown in the figure). Click OK.

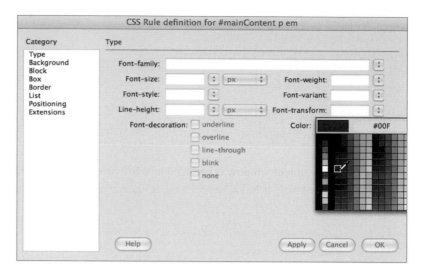

The emphasized sentence is now a new color.

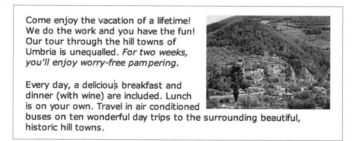

The style rules now contain a new rule that you can apply to any additional words, phrases, or sentences in a paragraph within the mainContent div. Just select the text you want to change and emphasize it by clicking the I button in the Properties panel.

You have used the Properties panel to create emphasized text and add new CSS rules to your styles. As you work through this book, you'll notice that Dreamweaver offers many kinds of Properties panels, in addition to those for text and graphics. Each element you select in the Document window will have a Properties panel appropriate to it. For this reason, most web designers leave the Properties panel window open at all times while they work.

Previewing a page in Live view

Live view allows you to preview your page in a live browser window from within Dreamweaver. Live view has additional features that will be explored in later lessons.

1   In the toolbar, click the Live View button. You may also press F11 (Windows) or Option+F11 (Mac) to enter Live view.

The display in the Document window is replaced by a live browser view. If the page includes elements such as links, JavaScripts, or Flash movies, they will be active in Live view.

2   To return to Edit mode, click the Live View button again, or press F11 (Windows) or Option+F11 (Mac) again.

Previewing pages in a browser

Although Dreamweaver does an excellent job of rendering web pages in the Document window and in Live view, it's important to always review your pages in one or more browsers. Dreamweaver allows you to preview your web page in any locally installed browser, once it has been identified in Preferences.

1   Choose File > Preview in Browser > Edit Browser List.

The Preferences dialog box appears, with the Preview in Browser category selected.

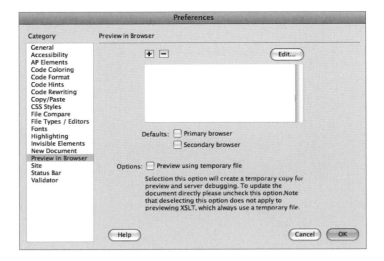

2 Click the Add button ⊞ to add a new browser to the list.

3 In the Add Browser dialog box, leave all fields blank and click Browse.

4 When the Select Browser dialog box opens, navigate to your preferred browser:

- To choose Firefox in Windows, navigate to Program Files > Mozilla Firefox > firefox. If Firefox is not installed in the Program Files folder, navigate your system to find it.

- To choose Internet Explorer in Windows, navigate to Program Files > Internet Explorer > iexplore.

- To choose Safari in Macintosh, navigate to Applications/Safari.

5 Click Open to confirm your choice.

● **Note:** Use the same method to add any additional browsers you may have. Viewing your pages in as many browsers as possible is a good testing practice.

6 In the Add Browser dialog box, in the Name field, type the name you want to appear in the browser list, such as **Firefox**, **Internet Explorer**, or **Safari** if necessary.

7 Select the "Primary browser" check box to pick the browser that will open when you press F12 (Windows) or Option+F12 (Mac) to preview in your preferred browser. Click OK.

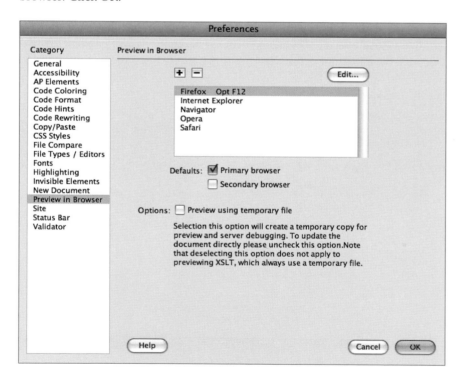

8 In the Preferences dialog box, click OK to complete the procedure.

9 Press F12 (Windows) or Option+F12 (Mac) to preview the current page in your primary browser. If you haven't saved the page, Dreamweaver will remind you to do so.

Clicking the Preview/Debug in Browser button 🌏 in the Document window allows you to preview in a browser other than your primary choice.

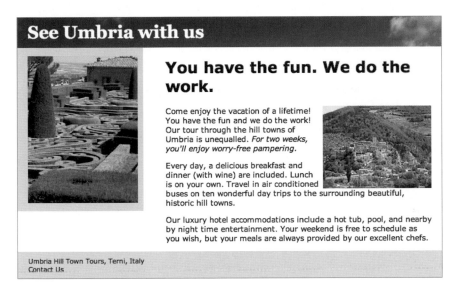

See Umbria with us

You have the fun. We do the work.

Come enjoy the vacation of a lifetime! You have the fun and we do the work! Our tour through the hill towns of Umbria is unequalled. *For two weeks, you'll enjoy worry-free pampering.*

Every day, a delicious breakfast and dinner (with wine) are included. Lunch is on your own. Travel in air conditioned buses on ten wonderful day trips to the surrounding beautiful, historic hill towns.

Our luxury hotel accommodations include a hot tub, pool, and nearby by night time entertainment. Your weekend is free to schedule as you wish, but your meals are always provided by our excellent chefs.

Umbria Hill Town Tours, Terni, Italy
Contact Us

10 After you've previewed your new web page, close your browser and return to Dreamweaver.

Congratulations—you've created your first web page in Dreamweaver. Using a Dreamweaver CSS layout, you have modified text, changed the colors, added images, added new CSS rules, and quickly produced a professional-looking web page. You have previewed the page in Live view and in a browser. As you can see, Dreamweaver combines substantial power with ease of use.

Review questions

1 How do you change the background color in the sidebar?

2 What two steps should you first perform when creating a new page from a CSS layout?

3 Name and briefly describe the four Dreamweaver views available in the Document window.

4 How do the two modes of the CSS Styles panel—All and Current—differ?

5 What happens when you toggle between HTML and CSS in the Properties panel? Why would you want to toggle between modes?

Review answers

1 Use the method you learned for changing the background color of the body. In the CSS panel, select the CSS rule .twoColFixHdr #sidebar1. Click the Edit button and select the Background category. Use the color picker to select a new color. Click OK.

2 Before you begin to modify the page appearance, change text, or modify CSS rules, you should change the page title and save the page.

3 Design view renders the current page like a browser. Code view displays the page's source code. Code and Design (Split) view shows both Design and Code views. Live view renders the page in a live interactive browser window.

4 The All mode displays a list of all styles associated with the current page, including those embedded in the <head> tag and those contained within external style sheets. The Current mode details the ways that a selected item on the page is affected by the page's style—providing a summary, a list of styles applied through inheritance in the Rules pane, and a Properties pane for the selected style (you'll learn more about this in Lesson 2). Styles can be edited using either mode.

5 Toggling between HTML and CSS displays selected page elements as either HTML or CSS properties. In some cases, you may want to see HTML properties to insert a link or add alternate text to an image. In other cases, you may want to see CSS properties to apply a CSS rule or to create a new CSS rule for the item selected.

2 WORKING WITH CASCADING STYLE SHEETS

In this lesson, you'll work with Cascading Style Sheets (CSS) in Dreamweaver and do the following:

- Attach an external style sheet

- Make a new CSS style rule

- Apply a style to your page

- Set up custom classes

- Use descendant selectors

- Create and style page layout elements

- Create a print style sheet

 This lesson will take about 60 minutes to complete. Be sure that you have copied the Lessons > lesson02 folder from the *Adobe Dreamweaver CS4 Classroom in a Book* CD to your hard drive before you begin. As you work on the lesson, you will save the start files using new names; so, if you need to restore the original file, you will have an unaltered version on your hard drive.

About Here and Back Travel

Meet our friendly staff

When you call our office in New York City, you will be connected to one of our experienced, helpful and friendly staff members. This is Here and Back Travel.

Elaine is the President and CEO of Here and Back Travel. She has 20 years experience in the travel industry and has traveled extensively to research the hotels and restaurants we recommend.

You may find her answering your phone calls or checking out a recommended hotel on Santorini.

Linda arranges all our organized tours to make traveling easy for those of you who like to have all the arrangements taken care of in advance. Linda is here to make your trip easy and restful so you can enjoy every minute.

Tours for people with special needs such as handicap access or special dietary needs are Linda's favorite to set up, so let Linda know if

The view from our offices in New York City.

Dreamweaver CS4 is a true CSS power tool with the ability to easily display, define, apply, and modify styles for a variety of media, including screen, print, and handheld devices.

Previewing a completed file

To see the finished page you will create in Lesson 2, you can preview it in a browser.

1   In the Files panel, expand the lesson02 folder.

2   Select the about-finished.html file, and press F12 (Windows) or Option+F12 (Mac).

● **Note:** The about-finished.html page is linked to the style sheet mystyles-finished.css.

3   Preview the page in your primary browser.

Note the layout and various styles applied to the text—all created by CSS styles.

About Here and Back Travel

The view from our offices in New York City.

Meet our friendly staff

When you call our office in New York City, you will be connected to one of our experienced, helpful and friendly staff members. This is Here and Back Travel.

Elaine is the President and CEO of Here and Back Travel. She has 20 years experience in the travel industry and has traveled extensively to research the hotels and restaurants we recommend.

You may find her answering your phone calls or checking out a recommended hotel on Santorini.

Linda arranges all our organized tours to make traveling easy for those of you who like to have all the arrangements taken care of in advance. Linda is here to make your trip easy and restful so you can enjoy every minute.

Tours for people with special needs such as handicap access or special dietary needs are Linda's favorite to set up, so let Linda know if you have any personal requirements.

Jason is our transportation expert and will set you up with the best transportation arrangements including airlines, trains, shuttles, ferries, and even car, motorcycle and bike rentals.

In addition to making sure you have your schedule and all your tickets, Jason also provides help with baggage transfers so your luggage will be waiting when and where you need it.

4   Close the browser and return to Dreamweaver to begin the lesson.

Attaching an external style sheet

In modern web design, it is considered a best practice to keep most of your CSS styles in external style sheets. Typically, all pages in a site should be linked to appropriate external style sheets. Doing so allows you to make a single style change—like changing the color of an <h1> tag—that will affect the entire site. Dreamweaver provides a straightforward way to attach an external style sheet to web pages.

1 If the Files panel is not on the screen, choose Window > Files.

2 In the Files panel, double-click lesson02 > about-start.html to open the page in the Document window.

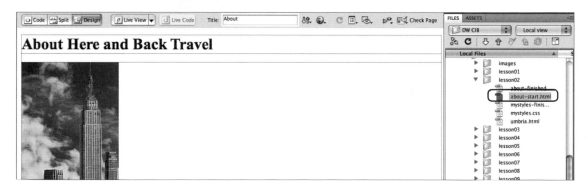

As you can see, the page has basic content—images, headings, and paragraphs—but no real layout or style. For this exercise, the entire layout and a good portion of the styles were previously created and stored in an external style sheet. Before you begin to work on the page, create a new version of it.

> **Note:** Files in the Files Panel of your DW CIB site may not exactly match the Files Panel figures shown throughout this book. File names mentioned in the exercises do precisely match your lesson files.

3 Choose File > Save As and save this page in the lesson02 folder using the name *about.html*.

The next task is to attach the external style sheet to the current page.

4 If necessary, choose Window > CSS Styles. In the CSS Styles panel, click Attach Style Sheet ⛓, the chain link icon at the bottom of the panel.

5 When the Attach External Style Sheet dialog box opens, click Browse. In the Select Style Sheet File dialog box, navigate to lesson02 and select mystyles.css. Click OK (Windows) or Choose (Mac).

> **Note:** Modern CSS allows for multiple media types, appropriate for screen, handheld, and print use. In this exercise, you first attach the external style sheet for the screen medium. Later in this lesson, you'll attach another style sheet for the print medium.

6 In the Attach External Style Sheet dialog box, verify that the Add as: Link option is selected. From the Media pop-up menu, choose screen. Click OK.

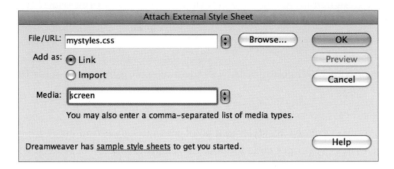

As you can see, the page has changed significantly. You will recognize the layout from Lesson 1. You can see the background image in the header that you used in Lesson 1 now repeated in the footer. The lower portion of the page is displayed in two columns.

7 Choose File > Save.

8 Click the Live View button, or press F12 (Windows) or Option+F12 (Mac) to preview the page in your primary browser. When you're done, click the Live View button again to return to Edit mode, or close your browser and return to Dreamweaver.

The lesson02 folder also contains an updated version of umbria.html in which the styles have been exported from the document <head> and a link added tying umbria.html and about.html to the same style sheet.

Site structure vs. lesson structure

As you proceed through the lessons, you'll notice that the mystyles.css file is included in every lesson folder. Your learning experience with each lesson depends on having a carefully prepared style sheet for each lesson.

When working on a site of your own design, it is normal to create a single style sheet and link to the same CSS file from every page on the site. Often a site will contain a folder called css that stores the various style sheets for screen, print, or other media.

In the next exercise, you'll create new style rules for your recently attached style sheet.

Creating new CSS rules

A CSS rule comprises two primary parts: a selector and one or more properties. For example, in the CSS rule below, the selector is the tag h1 and the properties are color: red and font-size: 36px:

```
h1 {
 color: red;
 font-size: 36px;
}
```

In Dreamweaver, you create CSS styles in a point-and-click environment, and Dreamweaver writes the proper code for you. As you grow more experienced with CSS, Dreamweaver also allows you to easily write CSS by hand. Dreamweaver allows you to define CSS rules for any selector type. In the next exercises, you'll create rules for two selector types: an HTML tag based on a descendant selector, and a custom CSS selector called a *class*.

Defining styles for descendant selectors

CSS rules that target specific tags are immediately and automatically applied whenever one of those tags is used. For example, in this exercise you'll create a rule for the <h1> tag in the mainContent div that changes the text color to blue, among other modifications. After this rule is defined, the text within any <h1> in the main-Content div will be blue for any page applying the same external style sheet.

1   If necessary, reopen the about.html file by double-clicking it in the Files panel.

2   In the CSS Styles panel, make sure that All mode is selected; if the panel is in Current mode, click All. Click the Plus (+) button (Windows) or expander arrow (Mac) next to the mystyles.css entry to expand it.

In Lesson 1, you saw these styles using the <style> syntax to indicate that the styles were in the document head. Here you see the filename–mystyles.css–of the external style sheet.

3   In the Document window, place your mouse pointer in the heading text, *Meet Our Friendly Staff*. Using the tag selector at the bottom of the Document window, select <h1>.

4   Click New CSS Rule ⬛, located at the bottom of the CSS Styles panel.

5   When the New CSS Rule dialog box opens, click the Less Specific button twice to choose the selector, #mainContent h1. Click OK.

The selector, #mainContent h1, is called a *descendant selector*. This rule will affect only <h1> tags descended from the #mainContent parent element. (The hash symbol (#) before mainContent designates that this division of the page was assigned the ID mainContent.) The <h1> tag in the #header area will not be affected. Descendant selectors may use an ID, such as #mainContent, or may be based on a class selector. You will create a class selector later in this lesson.

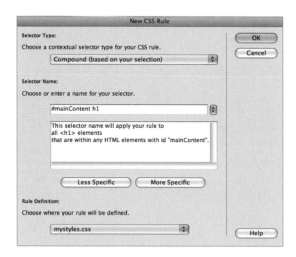

Initially, Dreamweaver inserts into the Selector field the selector associated with the current mouse pointer location. This feature is very useful when creating advanced selectors. For that reason, it's helpful to place your mouse pointer in the portion of the page where you're creating a style rule.

6   In the "CSS Rule Definition for #mainContent h1 in mystyles.css" dialog box, make sure the Type category is selected; if it isn't, choose Type from the Category column at the left of the dialog box.

7   In the Font-family pop-up menu, choose "Georgia, Times New Roman, Times, serif," or any similar available choice.

8   In the Color field, use the color picker to select a dark blue from the left edge of the graphic in the header. The color desired is #345FA3, although you may see a slightly different value. If you want exactly that color, type **#345FA3** in the Color field instead of using the color picker. Click OK.

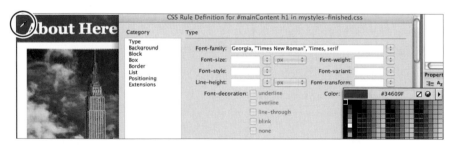

You changed the font family and color value for #mainContent <h1>. Should you add another <h1> to the mainContent area, it will follow the same rule. Since the file umbria.html is also linked to mystyles.css, the <h1> in the mainContent area of that page will also change. If you had a thousand pages linked to this style sheet, they would all instantly have a new font family and color for any #mainContent <h1> elements. It's a great example of the maintenance and updating advantages you gain from using an external style sheet.

Dreamweaver divides the available CSS properties into eight categories. Properties in the Type category affect the character formatting aspect of the selector.

9 Place your mouse pointer in the paragraph, *The view from our offices in New York City.* At the bottom of the Document window, select <p> in the tag selector.

10 At the bottom of the CSS Styles panel, click New CSS Rule ➕.

11 When the New CSS Rule dialog box opens, click Less Specific twice to choose the selector, #sidebar1 p. Click OK.

12 From the Category column, choose Type. In the Font-size field, type **80**, and from the pop-up menu, choose % From the Font-style pop-up menu, choose italic.

In Lesson 1, you used the I button on the Properties panel to create <em> text (which often renders in italics). In the current exercise, the font-style: italic rule creates italicized text with no <em> designation. In terms of HTML, the <em> adds emphasis, while font-style: italic is a decorative choice.

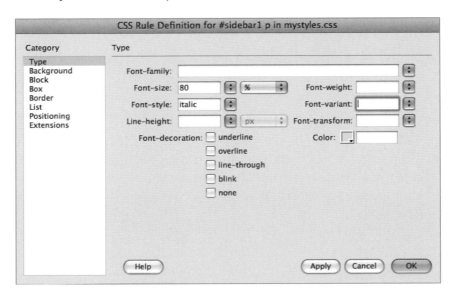

13 Choose the Box Category. In the Margin area, deselect the "Same for all" check box. In the Top field, type **0**. Click OK.

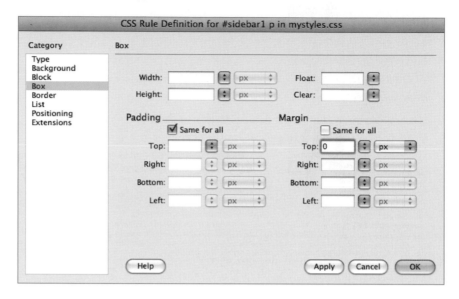

The Box category controls the invisible box surrounding elements by specifying values for its width, height, padding, margins, and other properties. This is often referred to as the *box model*. If the design called for the same amount of margin around the selector, you would have left the "Same for all" check box selected and typed a value in the Top field, which would also have been applied to Right, Bottom, and Left. Padding and margin values can be the same or different on each side of an element's surrounding box. Negative numbers are allowed too.

14 Choose File > Save All.

15 Preview the changes in Live view or in a browser.

Notice the changes you made to the <h1> heading and the paragraph under the image of New York City.

Note that the two new rules were added to the bottom of the All Rules list; this list reflects the order of the CSS rules in the style sheet. Designers often like to group related styles to make it easier to find them. The order of the rules in the style sheet also affects each rule's importance in the cascade. You can quickly move any style to a different location, and Dreamweaver will rewrite the code for you.

Meet our friendly staff

When you call our office in New York City, you will
one of our experienced, helpful and friendly staff
Here and Back Travel.

Elaine is the President and C
Back Travel. She has 20 years experience in the t
has traveled extensively to research the hotels an
recommend.

You may find her answering your phone calls or cl
recommended hotel on Santorini.

*The view from our offices in New
York City.*

16 In the CSS Styles panel, drag #mainContent
h1, the newly added style, under the
.twoColFixLtHdr #mainContent entry.

17 Drag #sidebar1 p to a position just under
.twoColFixLtHdr #sidebar1.

18 Choose File > Save All to store changes to
both the HTML and CSS files.

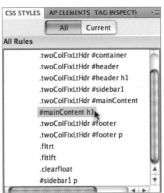

Setting up custom classes

Unlike descendant selectors that target a
particular tag in a specific context, not all CSS
rules are applied automatically. In the next exercise, you'll create a custom selector,
called a *class*, which can be applied as needed.

1 If necessary, open the about.html file by double-clicking its filename in the
Files panel.

2 At the bottom of the CSS Styles panel, click the New CSS Rule icon.

The New CSS Rule dialog opens.

3 In the Selector Type pop-up menu, choose Class (can apply to any HTML
element), and in the Selector Name field, type **.name**. Include the leading
period. Dreamweaver will insert it if you forget, but it's a good habit to acquire.
At some later time, you might insert a class into the style sheet manually and
you'll need the period.

4 Verify that the Rule Definition pop-up menu is set to mystyles.css, and click OK.

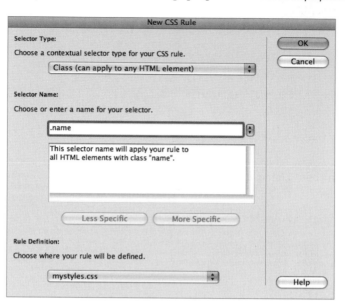

5 In the "CSS Rule Definition for .name in mystyles.css" dialog box, choose Type from the Category column. From the Font-variant pop-up menu, choose small-caps, and click OK.

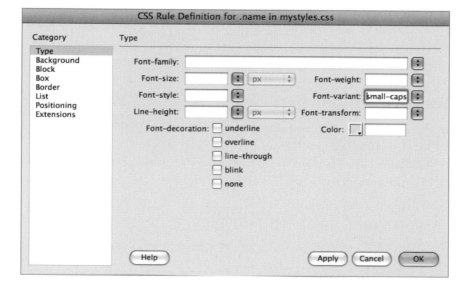

6 Choose File > Save All.

Having followed these steps, you won't notice any change in Dreamweaver other than finding another entry added to the All Rules list in the CSS Styles panel.

Because this rule uses a class selector, it must be applied manually—a process you'll perform in the next exercise.

Applying styles

Dreamweaver provides a variety of methods for applying a style to a tag. In this exercise, you'll use the Properties panel.

1 If necessary, open the about.html file by double-clicking its filename in the Files panel.

2 In the paragraph about Elaine, drag your mouse pointer across the first instance of the name *Elaine*.

The name and the area extending above it are highlighted.

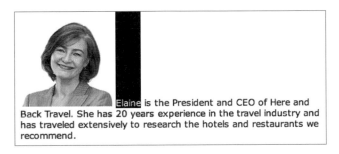

3 If necessary, press Control+F3 (Windows) or Command+F3 (Mac) to open the Properties panel. On the left side of the Properties panel, verify that the CSS button is selected.

4 From the Targeted Rule list of the Properties panel, choose .name.

Notice that the selected text is formatted as small caps and that the indicator in the tag selector includes the class name: `<span.name>`. The class was added to the selected text using a `<span>` tag.

As in this example, classes can be used within an existing tag (inline) to change a portion of an element (`<span>`), or they can be applied to override the default or CSS styling of the entire tag (`p`, `h1`, `div`, and so on).

● **Note:** The Properties panel's Targeted Rule list displays all the CSS classes that are available in a document. In addition, the inherited position of the rule in the cascade is shown.

5 To complete the page, repeat the process of highlighting the first instance of each person's name and then applying the .name class.

6 Preview the page using Live view or a browser.

Note that in Live view or a browser the small-caps formatting is rendered properly.

LIN manages our local recommendations department. She researches the reputation of every local restaurant, store, hotel, spa or other business that we recommend to our customers. She listens to returning travelers comments our recommended local businesses.

You can expect to hear from Lin when you return from a trip you planned with us. She will want to know what you thought of the accomodations, food, and places that you visited.

CHARLIE is our do-it-all guy. He takes care of the business end of things. He maintains this web site. He's also experienced at helping people make travel plans and can step in to help when everyone else is busy.

7 Click the Live View button again to return to Edit mode, or close your browser window and return to Dreamweaver.

8 Choose File > Save.

Applying custom classes to page divisions

Using Dreamweaver, you can easily insert page divisions, or <div> tags, into a document to create layout areas or to organize areas of a page. A <div> can be assigned an ID or a class. In this exercise, you will create several <div> sections and assign them all to the same custom class. These page divisions will allow you to float the images for each person. When floating elements, the clear property is often needed. Using the <div> sections also will give you an opportunity to use clear.

1 If necessary, open about.html by double-clicking its filename in the Files panel.

2 Use your mouse pointer to highlight Elaine's image and both paragraphs.

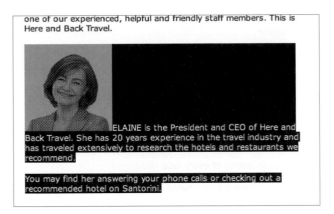

3 In the Insert panel, select Layout. Depending on your workspace configuration, you may see the Insert menu in a bar or a panel.

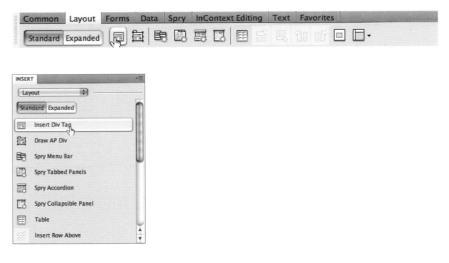

4 Choose Insert Div Tag.

The Insert Div Tag dialog box opens.

5 Be sure the Insert option is set to "Wrap around selection." In the Class field, type **.profile**.

6 Click the New CSS Rule button.

In the New CSS Rule dialog box, for the Selector Type, Class will already be chosen based on your selection.

7 In the Selector Name field, type **.profile**. In the Rule Definition pop-up menu, verify that the new rule will be located in the mystyles.css file. Click OK.

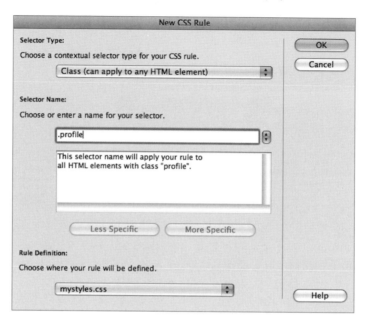

8 In the "CSS Rule Definition for .profile in mystyles.css" dialog box, from the Category column, choose Box. From the Clear pop-up menu, choose right.

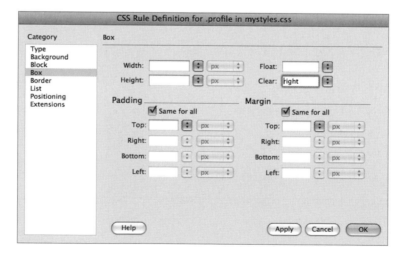

9 From the Category column, select Positioning. From the Overflow pop-up menu, choose auto. Click OK.

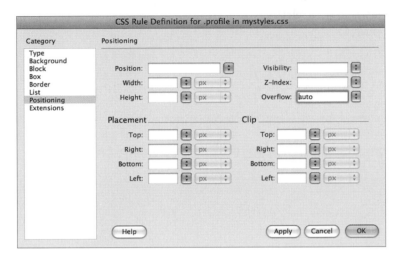

Later in this lesson, you will float the profile images. By using `clear:right` for `.profile`, each new div will find a clear space on the right margin to move to before creating a new <div.profile> element. As you learned in Lesson 1, when elements float, everything else wraps around them. To prevent the individual profiles from bumping into each other and wrapping awkwardly, the clear property is used.

Similarly, the overflow property is used in anticipation of another problem that float can cause. Without setting overflow to auto, the floated image might stick out of the bottom of the <div.profile> beyond where the text stops. To make the <div.profile> expand to contain the entire image and all the text, the overflow property is used.

10 Dreamweaver returns you to the Insert Div Tag dialog box. Click OK.

The Document window now displays a dotted line around the page section containing the selected picture and text, indicating the presence of a <div>. Until you make further changes to the page, you won't see any other differences in page appearance.

ELAINE is the President and CEO of Here and Back Travel. She has 20 years experience in the travel industry and has traveled extensively to research the hotels and restaurants we recommend.

You may find her answering your phone calls or checking out a recommended hotel on Santorini.

The process for adding similar <div> tags with the class .profile assigned will be slightly different for the other individuals on the page because the class .profile now exists in your mystyles.css file.

1 In the Document window, highlight the image of Linda and the two paragraphs about her.

2 In the Insert panel, from the Layout category, choose Insert Div Tag.

The Insert Div Tag dialog box opens.

3 From the Insert pop-up menu, choose "Wrap around selection" as you did previously. This time, however, you merely select your existing class, profile, from the Class menu to apply the class to the new <div>. Click OK.

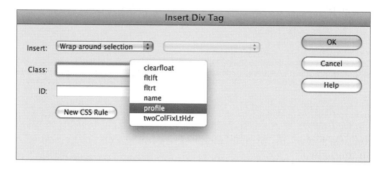

The section of the page devoted to Linda is now in its own <div>, which you can see reflected in the Document window by the dotted outline.

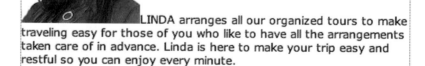

4 Repeat steps 1, 2, and 3 for the sections of the page about Jason, Lin, and Charlie.

5 Choose File > Save All to save both the page and the new CSS rules.

You created a separate layout division for each profile and assigned CSS class rules that will enable you to float the images in each profile in the next exercise.

Floating images

In the previous exercise, you created a class named .profile that set up rules for clear and overflow to the divs you added to the page. In the next exercise, you will use the float property to stagger the positions of the five profile images. With the rules you previously set up in .profile, you're ready for this exercise.

1 If necessary, open about.html by double-clicking its filename in the Files panel.

2 Select the image of Elaine. In the tag selector, make sure that the `<img>` tag is selected.

3 In the Properties panel, choose the class .fltrt.

Elaine's image now appears on the right, and the text about her wraps around the photo on the left.

4 Select the image of Linda. In the Properties panel, choose the class .fltlft.

Linda's image remains on the left, but because it is now floated, the text wraps around it on the right.

ELAINE is the President and CEO of Here and Back Travel. She has 20 years experience in the travel industry and has traveled extensively to research the hotels and restaurants we recommend.

You may find her answering your phone calls or checking out a recommended hotel on Santorini.

LINDA arranges all our organized tours to make traveling easy for those of you who like to have all the arrangements taken care of in advance. Linda is here to make your trip easy and restful so you can enjoy every minute.

Tours for people with special needs such as handicap access or special dietary needs are Linda's favorite to set up, so let Linda know if

5 Continue to float the remaining three profile images: Float Jason's image to the right, Lin's image to the left, and Charlie's image to the right.

6 Choose File > Save All to save your work.

7 Preview the page using Live view or a browser to see how the page displays the staggered small images and the text wrapped around each small image. Each profile begins in a clear space under the previous profile.

ELAINE is the President and CEO of Here and Back Travel. She has 20 years experience in the travel industry and has traveled extensively to research the hotels and restaurants we recommend.

You may find her answering your phone calls or checking out a recommended hotel on Santorini.

LINDA arranges all our organized tours to make traveling easy for those of you who like to have all the arrangements taken care of in advance. Linda is here to make your trip easy and restful so you can enjoy every minute.

Tours for people with special needs such as handicap access or special dietary needs are Linda's favorite to set up, so let Linda know if you have any personal requirements.

JASON is our transportation expert and will set you up with the best transportation arrangements including airlines, trains, shuttles, ferries, and even car, motorcycle and bike rentals.

In addition to making sure you have your schedule and all your tickets, Jason also provides help with baggage transfers so you

The view from our offices in New York City.

In the Properties panel, note that the available Targeted rule list now includes .profile. The rule could be applied to any element on the page using the Properties panel.

Cascade
body
.twoColFixLtHdr #container
.twoColFixLtHdr #mainContent
✓ .profile
New Rule
<New CSS Rule>
<New Inline Style>
▼

Examining selectors in the CSS Rules panel

In this exercise, you will take a closer look at the CSS Styles panel and learn some of the ways that Dreamweaver provides you with information about each style and its properties.

1 If necessary, open about.html by double-clicking its filename in the Files panel.

2 In the Document window, position your mouse pointer in one of the names that has the class .name applied to it.

3 In the CSS Styles panel, click All, then make sure the class .name is selected in the All Styles category, and click Current.

4 In the middle pane, click the icon to "Show information about the selected property" 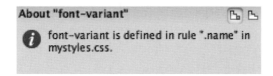, the leftmost of the two icons.

The About pane explains the origin of a particular style or property.

5 Select the "Show Cascade of rules for selected tag" icon to view the Rules pane instead of the About pane.

When you position your mouse pointer over a selector in the Rules pane, you'll see a tooltip conveying the same information available in the About pane, along with information about specificity that may help you with conflicts in the cascade.

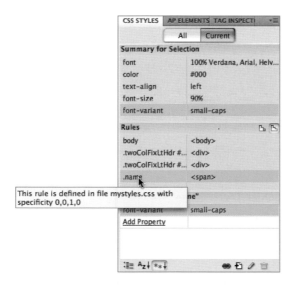

The Properties pane shows the properties for a selector. To see the Properties pane, you may need to drag down the bottom of the CSS Styles panel to lengthen it. The values can be edited directly in the Properties pane, and new properties can be added using the Add Property link.

> **Tip:** When conflicts are present, the CSS panel will strike through a selector name. Placing your mouse pointer over a selector that displays a strikethrough will display a tooltip that explains the conflict and may help you resolve it. The tooltip normally pops up over the Document window.

Creating style sheets for other media types

A key concept of modern web design is the separation of presentation (CSS) from content (the HTML tags, text, and other page elements). CSS files can present the content for a specific medium; for example, the style sheet applied in the previous exercises was designed to be displayed on a computer screen. In this exercise, you'll convert a CSS file for screen to a CSS file for print. Print style sheets often adjust colors to work better in print, hide unneeded page elements, or adjust sizes and layouts to be more suitable for printing.

More than one style sheet can be linked to a page. When a page is rendered for print, the printing device looks for a print media style sheet. If one is present, those CSS rules are taken into account. If not, the printer defers to the rules in the screen or all-media stylesheets. Similarly, handheld or Braille devices look for style sheets specific to that media. If they are present, the rules are used to render the page.

Displaying the Style Rendering toolbar

Dreamweaver's default display medium is screen media. However, Dreamweaver has the capacity to switch the media rendered in Design view using the Style Rendering toolbar. With Design view's rendering of the rules in a print style sheet, you can see the effect your style rules will have on a printed page.

1   If necessary, open the about.html file by double-clicking its filename in the Files panel.

2   Choose View > Toolbars > Style Rendering.

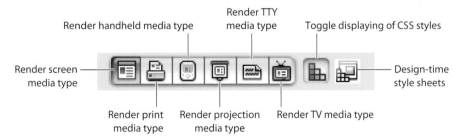

The Style Rendering toolbar appears above the Document window. Leave it visible for the next exercise.

Converting an existing style sheet for print

Although you can develop a print style sheet from scratch, it's usually much faster to convert an existing screen style sheet. The first step is to save the existing external style sheet under a new name.

1 In the Files panel, double-click mystyles.css to open it in Dreamweaver.

2 Choose File > Save As.

3 When the Save As dialog box opens, type **print.css** in the "File name" field, and click Save (Windows) or Save As (Mac).

4 If necessary, open the about.html file by double-clicking its filename in the Files panel.

5 In the CSS Styles panel, click Attach Style Sheet 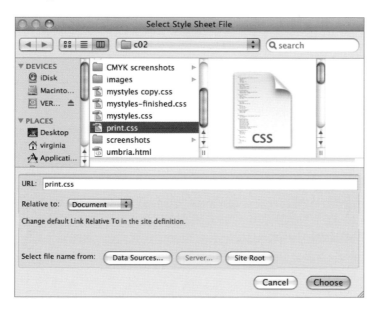. When the Attach External Style Sheet dialog box opens, click Browse.

The Select Style Sheet File dialog box appears.

6 In the Select Style Sheet File dialog box, navigate to the lesson02 folder and select print.css. Click OK (Windows) or Choose (Mac).

7 In the Attach External Style Sheet dialog box, verify that the Add as: Link option is chosen. From the Media pop-up menu, choose print, and click OK. In the CSS Styles panel, click All.

A new entry—print.css—has been added. You will change some of the print.css rules in the next exercise.

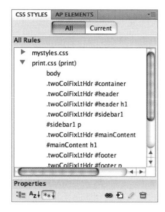

8 Close the print.css file in the Document window. In the about.html window, choose File > Save.

Hiding unwanted page areas

Using the Style Rendering toolbar, you can see your document rendered according to the print media style rules.

1 If necessary, open the about.html file by double-clicking its filename in the Files panel.

2 If necessary, choose View > Toolbars > Style Rendering.

3 In the Style Rendering toolbar, click the Render Print Media Type icon 🖨.

One of the main differences between screen and print media is that interactive items on a web page are often meaningless in print. This would include navigation elements, which you haven't yet added to about.html. For print media, you can hide unwanted portions of a page.

4 Place your mouse pointer anywhere in the #footer div.

5 In the CSS Styles panel, choose All. Find the style sheet print.css and expand it so that you can select .twoColFixLtHdr #footer.

6 In the CSS Styles panel, click Edit Rule.

7 When the "CSS Rule Definition for .twoColFixLtHdr #footer in print.css" dialog box opens, choose Block from the Category column. From the Display pop-up menu, choose none, and click OK.

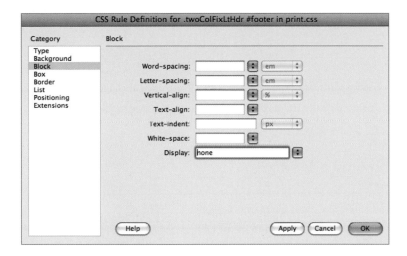

The footer is now hidden in the Document window when viewing the print media rendering. The display: none rule means that the div will not display in print.

Ensuring that colors work in print

Another item that might benefit from a change is the white text in the <h1> for the header that reads *About Here and Back Travel*. It might print well in white if the user's printer is set to print background images. If not, however, it might print as white text on white paper and therefore be invisible on the printed page

1 In the CSS Styles panel, select .twoColFixLtHdr #header h1. Click the Edit Rule icon .

2 In the "CSS Rule Definition for .twoColFixLtHdr #header h1 in print.css" dialog box, from the Category menu, choose Type.

3 Use the color picker to select the lightest shade of gray, #CCC, for Color. Click OK.

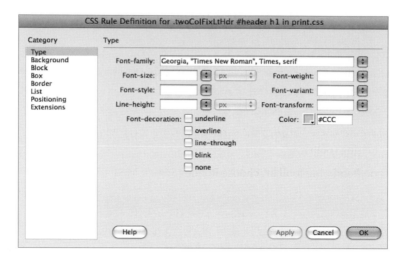

The text *About Here and Back Travel* will still be visible in print, whether or not the user's printer prints the dark background in the header area.

4 Choose File > Save All to save your work.

Removing unneeded styles

Currently, many styles in the print.css style sheet exactly match the same styles in the mystyles.css style sheet. To reduce file size, it is necessary to include only those rules that are new or changed from those in mystyles.css in the print.css style sheet. You can delete unneeded styles using the CSS Styles panel.

1 In the CSS Styles panel, highlight any selector, such as .twoColFixLtHdr #container, and click the Trash Can icon 🗑 to delete a rule.

Alternatively, in the Files panel, you can double-click print.css to open it in the Dreamweaver window where you can select and delete styles manually.

2 Highlight and delete all the styles except .twoColFixLtFtr #footer and .twoColFixLtHdr #header h1

When you finish, only two rules should remain in print.css: .twoColFixLtFtr #footer and .twoColFixLtHdr #header h1.

The print style sheet is ready to use. In this exercise, you made only two changes. Many other changes could be made in a print style sheet. For example, rules determining page width are often helpful. Printers don't understand pixels, so a print style sheet may use inches or points to measure width and font size.

To see the differences between the screen and print style sheets, you can use the Style Rendering toolbar.

3 In the Style Rendering toolbar, choose Render Screen Media Type 🖵 .

A printer (or other media device) reads both style sheets—you still see blue <h1> text in the mainContent area in print, for example. After a printing device reads the rules in mystyles.css, it moves on to read the rules in print.css. Since the rules in print.css come later, they overrule earlier rules.

4 Choose File > Save All. Then choose File > Close All.

You have adapted a screen media style sheet to make a web page render more usefully in print.

● **Note:** Another way to test your print style sheet is to preview the page in a browser and then choose File > Print; or, if no printer is available or you don't want to waste paper and ink, choose File > Print Preview (Windows), or choose File > Print and then choose Preview (Mac) in the Print dialog box.

Review questions

1　How do you attach an existing external style sheet to a web page?

2　What would be the difference in results between the CSS rules for the selector #header h1 and the selector #mainContent h1? What are these type of selectors called?

3　How do you apply a CSS class to a tag?

4　How do you insert new <div> areas into a web page?

5　What CSS property and value are used to hide any content associated with a CSS style?

Review answers

1　In the CSS Styles panel, choose Attach Style Sheet. In the Attach External Style Sheet dialog box, choose the desired CSS file and select the media type.

2　The rule for the selector #header h1 would apply only to an h1 located in a #header div. The rule for the selector #mainContent h1 would apply only to an h1 located in a #mainContent div. These selectors are known as *descendant selectors* because their application depends on being the descendant of a parent element in the document.

3　One method is to select the tag and then choose the style from the Properties panel's Style list.

4　In the Layout section of the Insert panel, choose Insert Div Tag. The new div can either surround selected content or be inserted into the document at the position of the mouse pointer.

5　Set the display property to none to hide any content you don't want to display.

3 WORKING WITH TEXT, LISTS, AND TABLES

In this lesson, you'll work with headings, paragraphs, and other text elements to do the following:

- Enter heading and paragraph text

- Insert text from another source

- Insert bulleted lists

- Insert blockquotes

- Check your spelling

- Search and replace text

- Insert and modify tables

- Use Spry tooltips

 This lesson will take about 60 minutes to complete. Be sure you have copied Lessons/lesson03 from the *Adobe Dreamweaver CS4 Classroom in a Book* CD to your hard drive before beginning. In the Lessons folder, place the lesson03 files in the lesson03 folder, and add the images to the images folder. An additional folder within the Lessons folder will be added as you complete lesson03. The new folder is SpryAssets.

See Santorini's Best

Santorini is perfect for beautiful oceans and fun-filled sunshine.

Paradise by the Sea

Welcome to Paradise! Santorini is Greece's most famous island for good reason. The scenic beauty, the stunning sunsets, the picturesque village and the friendly people all combine to create an unparalled vacation experience.

The Villages

Be sure to visit Fira, the capital, and nearby Oia. Both offer stunning

The web designer's world often revolves around text elements, which Dreamweaver creates with ease.

Previewing a completed file

To get a sense of the file you will work on in the first part of this lesson, let's preview the completed page in the browser.

1 Open Adobe Dreamweaver CS4.

2 If necessary, press F8 to open the Files panel, and choose DW CIB from the site list.

3 In the Files panel, expand the lesson03 folder.

4 Select the santorini-finished.html file and press F12 (Windows) or Option+F12 (Mac).

Note the variety of text elements used: headings, paragraphs, lists, tables and blockquotes, which are long sections of quoted text. Blockquotes are indented by default, as you see in the preview.

5 Close your browser and return to Dreamweaver.

Importing text

In this exercise, you enter heading and paragraph text imported from a text document.

1 In the Files panel, double-click the lesson03 > santorini-start.html file to open it.

2 Choose File > Save As and save the file as *santorini.html*. You'll work on this version of the file, leaving the original version unchanged.

You'll see a new page in the Here and Back Travel site. The images have been inserted, and you now need to work on the text.

3 In the Files panel, double-click the file santorini.txt to open it.

The text opens in the Dreamweaver Document window, where you can edit, copy, or paste the contents of the text file directly into a Dreamweaver HTML page.

```
####### paste under the first photo of the couple on the sunny rooftop######

Welcome to Paradise! Santorini is Greece's most famous island for good reason. The scenic beauty, the stunning sunsets, the picturesque
village and the friendly people all combine to create an unparalled vacation experience.

The Villages

Be sure to visit Fira, the capital, and nearby Oia. Both offer stunning sunsets, fine dining, and superlative shopping.

Stunning white-washed walls

Santorini blue cupolas

Colorful flowers

Historic sites everywhere you look

Olive groves dot the landscape

Eclectic shopping options please the most discerning shopper

Night life that just won't quit

The beaches
Beaches on every coast

No shortage of sandy fun

Swimming, water sports, boat tours

Amenities near the beaches include cafes, tavernas, umbrella rentals, parasailing, boat tours and more
```

4 Select all the text from "Welcome to Paradise! Santorini is. . ." to the end of that section, "Amenities near the beaches include cafes, tavernas, umbrella rentals, parasailing, boat tours and more."

```
####### paste under the first photo of the couple on the sunny rooftop######

Welcome to Paradise! Santorini is Greece's most famous island for good reason. The scenic beauty, the stunning sunsets, the picturesque
village and the friendly people all combine to create an unparalled vacation experience.

The Villages

Be sure to visit Fira, the capital, and nearby Oia. Both offer stunning sunsets, fine dining, and superlative shopping.

Stunning white-washed walls

Santorini blue cupolas

Colorful flowers

Historic sites everywhere you look

Olive groves dot the landscape

Eclectic shopping options please the most discerning shopper

Night life that just won't quit

The beaches
Beaches on every coast

No shortage of sandy fun

Swimming, water sports, boat tours

Amenities near the beaches include cafes, tavernas, umbrella rentals, parasailing, boat tours and more
```

5 Choose File > Copy, or press Control+C (Windows) or Command+C (Mac), to copy the selection.

6 At the top of the Document window, find the tab for the file santorini.html and click it to return to the web page.

7 Find and select the phrase *Add text here* located on the page immediately after the first image but before the second heading.

> Add text here
>
> ## What our customers say

8 Choose File > Paste, or press Control+V (Windows) or Command+V (Mac), to paste the new text into that location.

> Welcome to Paradise! Santorini is Greece's most famous island for good reason. The scenic beauty, the stunning sunsets, the picturesque village and the friendly people all combine to create an unparalled vacation experience.
>
> The Villages
>
> Be sure to visit Fira, the capital, and nearby Oia. Both offer stunning sunsets, fine dining, and superlative shopping.
>
> Stunning white-washed walls
>
> Santorini blue cupolas
>
> Colorful flowers
>
> Historic sites everywhere you look
>
> Olive groves dot the landscape
>
> Eclectic shopping options please the most discerning shopper

● **Note:** The pasted text was formatted as paragraphs in Dreamweaver because the santorini.txt file used two paragraph returns at the end of each section. If the original santorini.txt file contained only one paragraph return at the end of each section Dreamweaver's default formatting would have placed a line break <br /> at the end of each line.

By default, the pasted text is initially formatted with <p> tags, or as paragraphs. Note that the paragraphs are styled with the font choices already present in the style sheet. You can easily assign a basic format—such as an <h1>, <h2>, or <p> tag—to any text block using the Properties panel.

Before changing the formatting of this text, finish copying santorini.txt into the web page.

9 Click the santorini.txt tab to return to the text page.

10 Select the remainder of the page, beginning with "Dolores and Tom …"

11 Select and copy this text as you did in step 5.

12 Click the santorini.html tab to return to the web page.

13 Select the phrase *add text here* located after the photo of the building, but before the heading *Recommended Hotels*.

14 Paste the text into this location using the method you used in step 8.

15 In the santorini.txt tab, click the *x* symbol to close santorini.txt.

16 Choose File > Save to save your work.

Later in lesson03, you'll add a table to the last section of the page. First, you will format the new text you imported.

Creating headings, lists, and blockquotes

Text should be formatted to add meaning, organization, and clarity to content. In HTML terms, a heading tag—<h1>, <h2>, <h3>, <h4>, <h5>, and <h6>—creates a heading. Any browsing device, whether it is a computer, a Braille reader, or a cell phone, interprets text formatted with heading tags as a heading. Headings organize pages into meaningful sections with helpful titles in HTML pages, just as they do in books. In the same way, list tags and blockquote tags create formatting that carries with it additional meta-information that helps a user recognize text as a list or a long quote.

This concept applies to all HTML tags and is often referred to as semantic markup. The HTML tags create the semantic context for the page content: headings, paragraphs, lists, blockquotes, tables, images, and so on.

In this exercise, you'll do some basic semantic formatting using the Dreamweaver Properties panel.

1 If necessary, choose Window > Properties to open the Properties panel. Make sure that the HTML tab on the left is selected.

Because an external style sheet is already attached to this web page, the text takes on the assigned color, font, and size of the relevant CSS rule—all of which are displayed in the Properties panel when a section of text is selected.

It's easy to identify how the text is currently formatted.

2 Click in the heading *What our customers say*.

Notice that this is a Heading 2 (<h2>) element. You'll find that information displayed in the Properties panel and the tag selector.

Creating headings

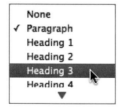

1 Scroll up the page a bit and click anywhere in the text *The Villages*.

2 In the Properties panel, make sure the HTML tab is selected. From the Properties panel Format menu, choose Heading 3.

The phrase "The Villages" is now formatted as a heading 3, or <h3>, element. This gives the phrase meaning and provides clarity and organization to the content following the heading.

3 Format the phrase *The Beaches* as a heading 3 element as well.

> ### The Villages
>
> Be sure to visit Fira, the capital, and nearby Oia. Both offer stu
> sunsets, fine dining, and superlative shopping.
>
> Stunning white-washed walls
>
> Santorini blue cupolas
>
> Colorful flowers
>
> Historic sites everywhere you look
>
> Olive groves dot the landscape
>
> Eclectic shopping options please the most discerning shopper
>
> Night life that just won't quit
>
> ### The Beaches

Creating lists

Lists are the workhorses of the web because they are easier to read than blocks of dense text and also help users find answers quickly. In this exercise, you will make an unordered list.

1 Select all the incomplete sentences following the sentence *Both offer stunning sunsets, fine dining, and superlative shopping.*

> ### The Villages
>
> Be sure to visit Fira, the capital, and nearby Oia. Both offer stu
> sunsets, fine dining, and superlative shopping.
>
> Stunning white-washed walls
>
> Santorini blue cupolas
>
> Colorful flowers
>
> Historic sites everywhere you look
>
> Olive groves dot the landscape
>
> Eclectic shopping options please the most discerning shopper
>
> Night life that just won't quit
>
> ### The Beaches

2 With the text selected, click the Unordered List button in the Properties panel.

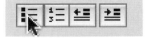

● **Note:** If you needed to create an ordered list, you would click the Ordered List button, the button with numbers.

These buttons are toggles. If you type your own list and want to stop using the list format, click the list button to return to the default paragraph formatting.

● **Note:** In HTML code, a numbered list is designated by the tag <ol>, or ordered list. A bulleted list uses the tag <ul>, or unordered list. Notice that these lists appear in the tag selector with the tags <ul> representing the entire list and <li> representing individual list items.

3 Repeat the steps for all the text following the heading *The Beaches*.

The Villages

Be sure to visit Fira, the capital, and nearby Oia. Both offer stunning sunsets, fine dining, and superlative shopping.

- Stunning white-washed walls
- Santorini blue cupolas
- Colorful flowers
- Historic sites everywhere you look
- Olive groves dot the landscape
- Eclectic shopping options please the most discerning shopper
- Night life that just won't quit

The Beaches

- Beaches on every coast
- No shortage of sandy fun
- Swimming, water sports, boat tours
- Amenities near the beaches include cafes, tavernas, umbrella rentals, parasailing, boat tours and more

---

4 Choose File > Save.

Lists can be styled many ways in Dreamweaver CS4. The navigation you will add to the pages in Lesson 5 will give you experience with styled lists, so you'll leave these lists in their default styles.

Creating blockquotes

A blockquote in HTML is literally a block of quoted text. We'll move down the page to the section called *What our customers say* to create blockquotes.

1 Place your mouse pointer anywhere in the paragraph that begins *We loved Santorini more....*

2 In the Properties panel, click the button for blockquotes.

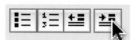

The tooltip calls it "Text Indent," which is not quite an accurate description. This button actually creates an HTML blockquote. To return to normal paragraph formatting following a blockquote when manually typing content in the page, click the Text Outdent button just to the left of the Text Indent button.

3 Repeat step 2 for the paragraphs beginning *The food at the little bistro...* and *My whole family....*

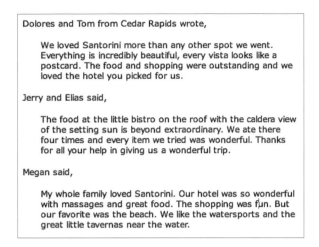

Dolores and Tom from Cedar Rapids wrote,

We loved Santorini more than any other spot we went. Everything is incredibly beautiful, every vista looks like a postcard. The food and shopping were outstanding and we loved the hotel you picked for us.

Jerry and Elias said,

The food at the little bistro on the roof with the caldera view of the setting sun is beyond extraordinary. We ate there four times and every item we tried was wonderful. Thanks for all your help in giving us a wonderful trip.

Megan said,

My whole family loved Santorini. Our hotel was so wonderful with massages and great food. The shopping was fun. But our favorite was the beach. We like the watersports and the great little tavernas near the water.

Now, you'll style those blockquotes with a new CSS rule.

4 In the CSS panel, click the New CSS Rule icon.

5 In the New CSS Rule dialog box, choose "Tag (redefines an HTML element)" from the Selector Type pop-up menu. In the Selector Name field, type **blockquote**. (Alternatively, use the pop-up menu by the Selector Name field to choose blockquote.) In the Rule Definition pop-up menu, verify that the new style will be defined in mystyles.css. Click OK.

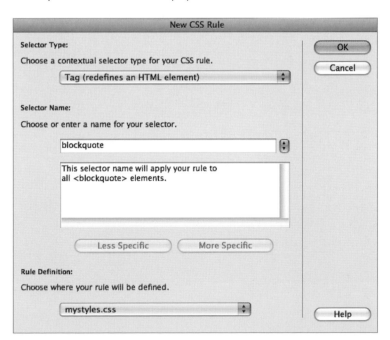

6 In the "CSS Rule Definition for blockquote in mystyles.css" dialog box that opens, from the Category column, choose Box. In the Padding area, deselect the "Same for all" check box; in the Right and Left fields, type **4**, and in the unit options pop-up menus for Right and Left, choose px.

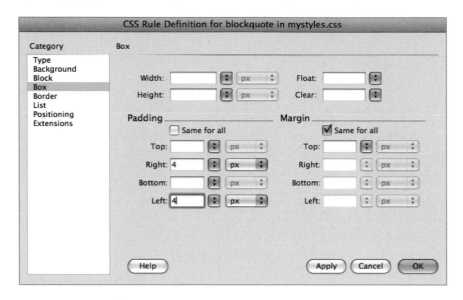

7 Select the Border category. In the pop-up menus in the Style section, choose solid, and in the Width section choose thin. Under Color, click the color box to open the color picker .Select the dark blue #00C. Click OK.

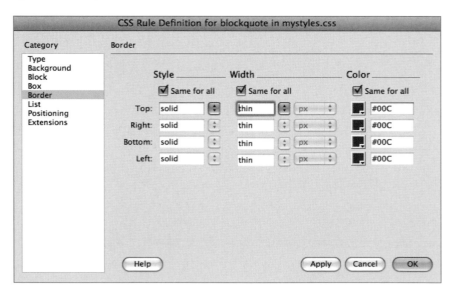

8 Choose File > Save All to save both the HTML and the CSS pages.

9 Use Live view or preview in a browser to see your progress.

Creating tables

In the early days of the web, pages were laid out with tables instead of CSS. Many browsing devices interpret tables as what they actually are—rows and columns of data—rather than as a comprehensible page layout. When CSS came along, people came to believe that "tables are bad" because pages should be laid out with CSS. That was a bit of an overreaction. Tables are not good for page layout, but they are very good, and very necessary, for displaying rows and columns of data.

1 If necessary, use the Files panel to open the file santorini.html in the lesson03 folder.

2 Scroll to the bottom of the page, to where you see the text *Add a table here*. Delete that text and leave your mouse pointer in that position.

3 In the Insert panel, click the Layout tab, and then click the Table icon. If you are using the Insert panel, rather than the classic bar arrangement, the visual appearance of the Layout category will be slightly different. The table icon appearance is the same in both.

4 In the Table dialog box, type **6** for Rows and **3** for Columns. Ensure that width, border, padding, and spacing are left blank.

These presentation aspects of the table will be created in CSS, making the table more accessible and useful on many devices in addition to the computer screen.

5 In the Header section, choose Top, so that headings will be set at the top of each column, and in the Caption field, type *Santorini Hotels*. Click OK.

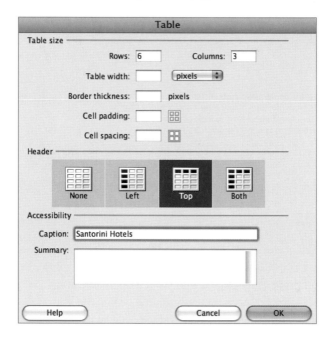

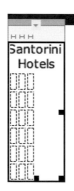

The table appears in the Dreamweaver document in a squished and unimpressive format, because it currently contains no content and has no size applied.

Using the Properties panel, you can assign an ID to the table.

6 In the Table field, type **hotels**.

7 Click in the first cell of the top row of the table. Type **Town**.

8 Press the Tab key to move to the next cell in the row. Type **Hotel**.

9 Press Tab once more and type **Rating**.

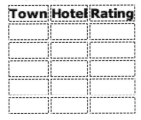

To save time, you'll copy and paste a completed table.

10 In the Files panel, find the file table.html and double-click it to open it.

11 Click anywhere inside the table and select `<table#hotels>` in the tag selector.

Santorini Hotels		
Town	**Hotel**	**Rating**
Fira	Mikel's Suites Luxury Hotel	****
Oia	Rota's Spa Hotel of Oia	****
Imerovigli	Greco Luxury Suites	****
Fira	Fira Luxury Traditional Houses	****
Kamari	Eros Hotel Resort & Spa	****

12 Choose Edit > Copy, or press Control+C (Windows) or Command+C (Mac), to copy the table.

13 Close the table.html tab and return to the santorini.html page.

14 Select the `<table#hotels>` tag to select the entire table, then press Delete to delete the incomplete table that you began.

Note: It is not absolutely necessary to assign an ID to the table in this exercise because one table will be placed on the page. However, if you have more than one table on a page, assigning an ID to each table allows you to create individual styles for each table. In the same manner, IDs can be assigned to lists, blockquotes, or any other page element using the Properties panel.

Note: In step 5, you set up the table with the first row at the top to contain table headers, or `<th>` tags. Notice that they are bold by default. Although you can't see it in this shrink-wrapped table, the `<th>` tags are also centered by default. Click an empty cell below any of the table headers and you'll see a `<td>` tag, for table data. The other table elements you'll see in the tag selector include `<table#hotels>` and `<tr>`. The table itself can be selected using `<table#hotels>`, while `<tr>` is a table row. Click in the caption text and you will see `<caption>` displayed in the tag selector.

15 Choose Edit > Paste, or press Control+V (Windows) or Command+V (Mac), to paste the complete table onto the page.

16 Choose File > Save.

Styling tables with CSS

Dreamweaver's CSS tools make it easy to present tables in a multitude of ways. In this exercise, you will create CSS rules to control the size of a table and add borders.

1 If necessary, open the file santorini.html by double-clicking the filename in the Files panel.

2 Locate the table near the bottom of the page.

3 Click anywhere in the table. Then use the tag selector to select `<table#hotels>`.

4 With the table selected, in the CSS Styles panel, click the New CSS Rule button 🗐.

5 In the New CSS Rule dialog box, choose Tag (redefines an HTML element) from the Selector Type pop-up menu. Dreamweaver will automatically place *table* in the Selector Name field based on your current selection in the Document window. In the Rule Definition pop-up menu, verify that the new rule will be defined in mystyles.css. Click OK.

▶ **Tip:** When a table is selected, the Properties panel allows you to quickly make changes to that table, such as adding a new row or column. Table-based spacing, padding, and borders, are best handled in CSS as you will do in the next exercise. You can also add or remove table rows and columns in the Modify menu.

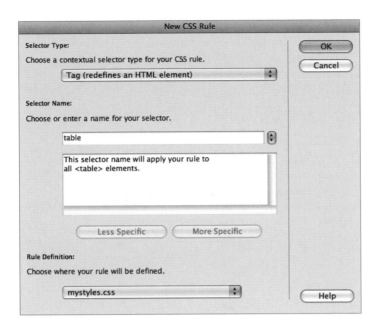

This step adds the selector *table* to the mystyles.css file. Next you will create rules for the new selector.

6 In the "CSS Rule Definition for table in mystyles.css" dialog box, choose Box from the Category column. In the Width field, type **475**, and choose px in the unit options pop-up menu. In the Padding area, in the Top field, type **4**, and the value will autofill to all sides of the box.

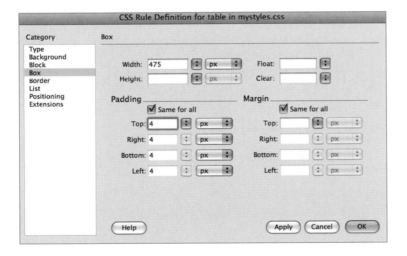

7 Choose Border from the Category column. In the pop-up menus, choose solid in the Style area, thin in the Width area, and #00C in the Color area. The values should automatically complete for Top, Right, Bottom, and Left. Click OK.

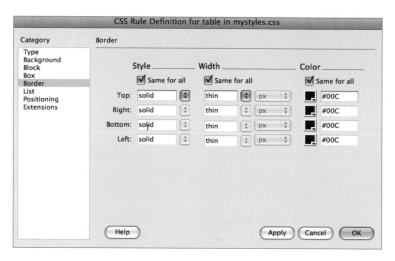

8 Choose File > Save All. Use Live view or a browser to preview the page.

You will see that the size and padding around the text have changed. A border has been placed around the table, but not around the individual table cells. Notice that the table caption is not enclosed within the table borders.

Santorini Hotels		
Town	**Hotel**	**Rating**
Fira	Mikel's Suites Luxury Hotel	✶✶✶✶
Oia	Rota's Spa Hotel of Oia	✶✶✶✶
Imerovigli	Greco Luxury Suites	✶✶✶✶
Fira	Fira Luxury Traditional Houses	✶✶✶✶
Kamari	Eros Hotel Resort & Spa	✶✶✶✶

9 Click Live View again or close the browser window to return to Dreamweaver.

10 Click the New CSS Rule button to create a new style.

In the New CSS Style Rule dialog box, you will create a list of selectors separated by commas.

11 From the Selector Type pop-up menu, choose Compound (based on your selection). Delete everything in the Selector Name field, and type **th, td**.

12 Ensure that the new rule will be defined in mystyles.css. Click OK.

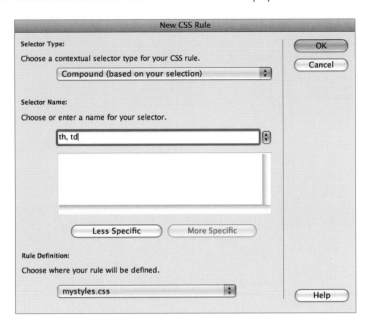

13 In the "CSS Rule Definition for th, td in mystyles.css" dialog box, choose Border from the Category column. Enter the same values (solid, thin, #00C) that you used for the table border. Click OK.

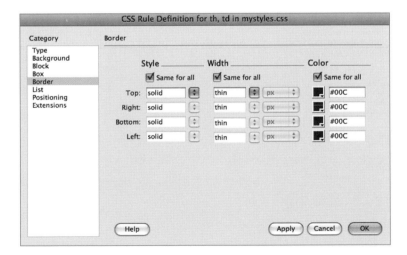

Your final step is to eliminate the gap between the table cells' border lines. Dreamweaver's CSS Rule Definition dialog box does not include the property needed for this CSS rule, so you will add it manually using the CSS Styles panel.

14 In the CSS Styles panel, click the All tab, and then, in the All Rules pane, choose the table selector. In the Properties for "table" pane, click Add Property.

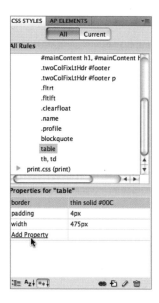

15 Type the property **border-collapse**. Press Tab to move to the value field and type **collapse**. Press Enter (or Return) to confirm the new property and value.

16 Choose File > Save All to save all your work.

17 Examine your work using Live view or a browser.

Santorini Hotels

Town	Hotel	Rating
Fira	Mikel's Suites Luxury Hotel	****
Oia	Rota's Spa Hotel of Oia	****
Imerovigli	Greco Luxury Suites	****
Fira	Fira Luxury Traditional Houses	****
Kamari	Eros Hotel Resort & Spa	****

Although the table is still pretty plain, setting a width and adding borders in CSS has made it much easier to read and understand. CSS rules could be applied to `<caption>`, `<table>`, `<tr>`, `<th>`, `<td>` and other table elements to further enhance the appearance.

Spell-checking a document

It's important to ensure that the content you post to the web is error free. Dreamweaver includes a robust spell checker capable of identifying commonly misspelled words and creating a custom dictionary.

1 If necessary, open the santorini.html file by double-clicking its entry in the Files panel.

2 Click in the `<h1>` heading, *See Santorini's Best*.

3 Choose Commands > Check Spelling.

● **Note:** Dreamweaver starts the spell check from the current mouse pointer position and, when it reaches the end of the document, offers to start again from the top, if necessary. By positioning the pointer at the top of the document, you avoid this step.

When the Check Spelling dialog box appears, it immediately flags the first error it encounters, or the first word not present in your personal dictionary.

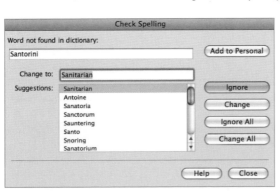

To replace an incorrectly spelled word with the word currently selected in the Suggestions field, click Change. Or select the correct word in the Suggestions field and click Change.

Dreamweaver then moves to the next questionable word.

If you know the current word is spelled correctly—for example, the word *Santorini* is correct in this example—click Ignore. Click Add to Personal to add the word to your personal dictionary so that Dreamweaver will not flag it on future references.

If none of the suggested words in the Check Spelling dialog box match the proper spelling of a word, you can type the correct word in the "Change to" field and click Change.

4 Repeat this process until all the questioned words are either added to the personal dictionary or replaced. Dreamweaver will question the Greek names, but they are all spelled correctly. When Dreamweaver displays a note indicating that the spelling check is complete, click OK. If Dreamweaver offers to continue the spelling check from the start of the document, click No.

5 Choose File > Save.

Using the Spry Tooltip widget

Dreamweaver CS4 includes a Spry Tooltip widget that allows you to control the placement and appearance of a tooltip. In HTML, a tooltip is created using a title attribute with a tag such as `<acronym>`. However, the Dreamweaver CS4 Spry tooltip uses JavaScript and CSS.

1 If necessary, open the santorini.html file by double-clicking its entry in the Files panel.

2 In the table, select the word *Oia* under the heading *Town*.

3 In the Spry category on the Insert panel, select the Spry Tooltip icon.

4 Scroll to the bottom of the Document window. Find the "Spry Tooltip: sprytooltip1" area. Delete the text *Tooltip content goes here* and type *Oia is pronounced Eea*.

5 Choose File > Save.

6 If this is the first Spry tooltip in your site, a Copy Dependent Files dialog box may notify you that two files will be added to your site. Click OK. You may not see this dialog box because the files were already present for the preview page at the opening of this chapter.

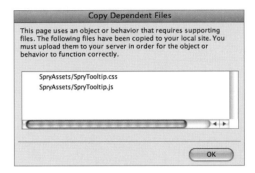

7 Click the tooltip label, "Spry Tooltip: sprytooltip1," to select the tooltip so you can familiarize yourself with the Properties panel options for controlling the tooltip settings for things like offsets, delays, effects, and mouse actions. Don't change anything at this time.

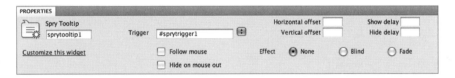

8 In the CSS Styles panel, make sure that the All tab is selected. Scroll to the bottom of the All Rules pane to find the new SpryTooltip.css file that was attached to your page. Click the Plus (+) button (Windows) or expander arrow (Mac) to expand the SpryTooltip.css contents.

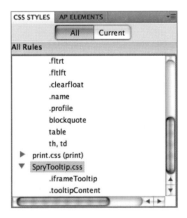

▶ **Tip:** Each Spry widget you use puts a CSS file and a JavaScript file into the folder called SpryAssets in your site root folder. Be sure to upload the folder containing all these files when you publish your site. When you added the SpryAssets folder to your Dreamweaver CIB folder to prepare to work in this book, many of these JavaScript and CSS files were already present. During the book exercises, you may notice that the files have been linked to your page, but you may not see the Copy Dependent Files dialog box.

9 Select .tooltipContent and click the pencil icon to edit the CSS rule.

10 In the "CSS Rule Definition for .tooltipContent in SpryTooltip.css" dialog box, select Background from the Category column. Change Background-color to #345FA3 to match the color in the <h2> headings. The heading color was changed in mystyles.css in Lesson 1. Click OK.

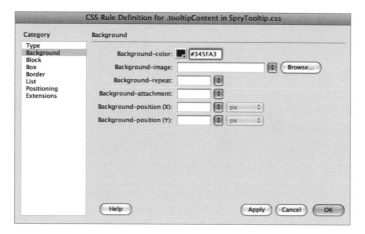

11 Choose File > Save All to save everything.

12 Use Live view or a browser to try out the tooltip. You must position the mouse pointer near the word Oia to see the tooltip.

Santorini Hotels

Town	Hotel	Rating
Fira	Mikel's Suites Luxury Hotel	★★★★
Oia	Rota's Spa Hotel of Oia	★★★★
Imerovig Oia is pronounced Eea		★★★★
Fira	Fira Luxury Traditional Houses	★★★★
Kamari	Eros Hotel Resort & Spa	★★★★

13 Click Live View again or close your browser to return to Edit mode in Dreamweaver.

You added a Spry Tooltip to a widget to create a tooltip in which placement and appearance can by styled using CSS.

Finding and replacing text

The ability to find and replace text is one of Dreamweaver's most powerful features. Designers can target any amount of text—white space, hard returns, spaces, and other textual elements—from a selection in the current document to an entire site. You can search just the rendered text on the page, the underlying tags, or both. Advanced users can enlist powerful pattern-matching algorithms called *regular expressions* to perform the most sophisticated find-and-replace operations.

In this exercise, you'll find and replace a single phrase in the current document.

1 If necessary, open the santorini.html file by double-clicking its entry in the Files panel.

2 Choose Edit > Find and Replace. When the Find and Replace dialog box opens, from the "Find in" pop-up menu, choose Current Document. From the Search pop-up menu, choose Text.

You'd do well to familiarize yourself with the options in both the "Find in" and Search menus. The "Find in" menu controls the scope of the search—available options include selected text, code, current document, the open documents, a specified folder, documents chosen in the Files panel, and the current site. The Search menu determines the type of search—the Source Code, the text in Design view, text located within set code, or specific tags.

In this exercise, you'll search for the word *shopper* and replace it with the word *buyer*.

3 In the Find field, type **shopper**, and click Find Next.

Dreamweaver locates the first instance of the phrase.

By clicking the Find Next button, you can examine each found instance and determine if it should be replaced.

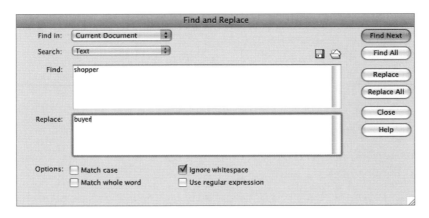

4 In the Replace field, type **buyer**, and click Replace.

Dreamweaver replaces the first instance of the found phrase and immediately searches for the next instance. When every instance of the word has been found, Dreamweaver inserts a small notice at the bottom of the dialog box that tells you that there are no more instances of the word. Click Close.

You imported text to a web page and formatted it as headings, paragraphs, lists, and blockquotes. Then, you created a table and inserted a tooltip in the table. You've reviewed text using Dreamweaver's Spell Check and Find and Replace tools, and you styled a blockquote, table, and tooltip using CSS.

Review questions

1 How do you format a Heading 1 or Heading 2?

2 Explain an easy way to copy and paste content from a text file into a Dreamweaver web page.

3 In this lesson, you created an unordered list. How might you create an ordered list of the top ten things to do in Santorini for this page?

4 How do you style a table caption?

5 What kinds of search-and-replace operations are available in Dreamweaver?

6 How might you add a tooltip to the table that informs users that *Fira* is often spelled *Thera*? What controls the way this tooltip is styled?

Review answers

1 Use the Properties panel to assign <h1> through <h6> tags to headings.

2 Dreamweaver is able to open simple text files, from which text can be copied and pasted into the Web page.

3 Type the text for the list in Dreamweaver's Document window, select it all, and click the Ordered List button in the Properties panel. Or, in the Properties panel, click the Ordered List button, type the list, and click the Ordered List button once again to turn off the list formatting.

4 Create a new CSS rule for the tag caption and style it as desired.

5 Dreamweaver can search the text in Design view, the underlying code, or both. The scope of the search can encompass a block of selected text, the current page, a folder of pages, or the entire site.

6 Use the same technique used to add the first tooltip. Select a word, and in the Spry category of the Insert panel, click the Spry Tooltip button. Scroll to the bottom of the document window to edit the tooltip text. The new tooltip would be styled according to the rules in the file SpryTooltip.css and should reflect your change to the background color.

4 WORKING WITH IMAGES

In this lesson, you'll include images in your web pages in the following ways:

- Inserting an image

- Applying a background image

- Using Bridge to import Photoshop or Fireworks files

- Copying and pasting an image from Photoshop

- Using Photoshop Smart Objects

 This lesson will take about 60 minutes to complete. Be sure you have copied Lessons > lesson04 from the *Adobe Dreamweaver CS4 Classroom in a Book* CD onto your hard drive before beginning.

Charming Naxos

Naxos is a large island with charming seaside villages, mountain villages, hiking trails, and wonderful fresh seafood.

The essential Greek isle

The large island of Naxos has something for everyone. Wander the capital of Chora and enjoy the seaside dining, the fishing boats, the delightful shops and the nearby beaches.

Walk through the warren of wonderful shops and resturants to the castle atop the hill. It's a fairyland at night.

A short stretch from Chora's seaside restaurant row to the marble Portera marking the site of an abandoned temple is a lovely stroll at

Dreamweaver provides many ways to work with graphics, both within the program and in tandem with other graphics tools such as Adobe Fireworks CS4 and Adobe Photoshop CS4.

Previewing the completed file

To get a sense of the file you will work on in this lesson, let's preview the completed page in the browser.

1 Open Adobe Dreamweaver CS4.

2 If necessary, press F8 to open the Files panel, and choose DW CIB from the site list.

3 In the Files panel, expand the lesson04 folder.

4 Select the naxos-finished.html file and press F12 (Windows) or Option+F12 (Mac) to preview the page in your primary browser.

   The page includes several images, both foreground and background, as well as a Photoshop Smart Object image.

5 Close your browser and return to Dreamweaver.

Inserting an image

Images are key components of any web page. The Insert panel has a number of buttons that make inserting an image fast and easy. You can also add Image Placeholders or replace Image Placeholders with images, as in the first exercise.

1 In the Files panel, expand the lesson04 folder and double-click the naxos-start. html filename to open the file.

2 Choose File > Save As and save the file in the lesson04 folder using the filename *naxos.html*. That way, if you need to refer to the naxos-start.html page, it will be preserved in its original form on your hard drive.

In some cases, image placeholders have been used to indicate where some of the graphics will be inserted during this lesson. Elsewhere, an empty space has been reserved for an image.

3 Select the image placeholder labeled "potara (200 × 200)," and press Delete to remove it.

4 Choose the Common category of the Insert panel, and click the Image icon .

If you don't see the Image icon in the Insert panel, click the down arrow next to the Images button and choose Image. Like other menus accessed through the Insert panel, the Images menu displays the most recently chosen object as the first item.

5 When the Select Image Source dialog box appears, navigate to the images folder and select naxos-portara.jpg. Click OK (Windows) or Choose (Mac).

6 In the Image Tag Accessibility Attributes dialog box, in the Alternative Text field, type **Naxos Portara** and click OK.

An alternative technique for adding an image to the page is to use the Assets panel.

7 Delete the naxos-portara.jpg image you just added.

8 Choose Window > Assets. When the Assets panel opens, click the Images category icon, the top icon in the column on the left of the panel.

9 Scroll down to locate and select the naxos-portara.jpg image.

● **Note:** You can also double-click a placeholder image to open the Select Image Source dialog box and exchange the placeholder for an actual graphic. Using this method, you will have to type alt (alternative) text manually in the Properties panel Alt field because this image placeholder does not include alt text.

Naxos is a large island with charming seaside villages, mountain villages, hiking trails, and wonderful fresh seafood.

The panel lists the image name, dimensions in pixels, and file type as well as its path. You may need to enlarge the panel if you want to see all the information.

10 At the bottom of the panel, click the Insert button to insert the image at your current mouse pointer location. Dreamweaver also allows you to drag the image icon from the panel to the page, if you prefer.

11 In the "Image Tag Accessibility Attributes" dialog box, type **Naxos Portara**. Click OK.

12 Choose File > Save.

Using image placeholders

Image placeholders are a great tool for developing web pages when the final images are not available. An image placeholder is rendered in Dreamweaver using a plain gray rectangle with a title and the dimensions of the intended image. Image placeholders are intended for design time only. If the page is previewed in a browser, the image placeholders do not appear, although some browsers—such as Microsoft Internet Explorer—indicate a missing figure. To insert an image placeholder, follow these steps:

1 Place your mouse pointer where you want the image placeholder to appear.

2 In the Common category of the Insert panel, select Image Placeholder using the Images menu.

3 When the Image Placeholder dialog box opens, type the name of the object in the Name field.

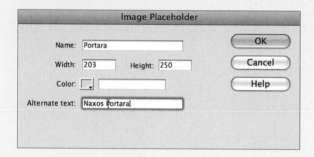

● **Note:** The name should not include spaces or special characters. Mixed-case names, like ourHouse, or names with underscores, such as Our_House, are permitted.

4 Type the desired image width in the Width field and the height in the Height field.

Once the placeholder has been inserted, it can be resized in Design view at any time.

5 If you'd prefer a color other than the default gray, click the color box and choose a new color from the color picker.

6 Enter the alt text for the intended image in the Alternative text field, and click OK.

To replace the placeholder image with an actual graphic, double-click the placeholder image and choose your desired image from the Select Image Source dialog box. Both the name and alt text attribute values will be carried over from the image placeholder to the newly inserted image.

Using background images

Web pages can incorporate two types of images: foreground and background. Foreground images are web graphics (in JPG, GIF, or PNG format) that are added to the document using an <img> tag. You inserted a foreground images in the previous exercise. Background images, on the other hand, are included in the page using CSS.

1 If necessary, open the naxos.html file by double-clicking its entry in the Files panel.

2 Choose Window > CSS Styles and, if necessary, click All to enter All mode.

3 In the mystyles.css listing, select .twoColFixLtHdr #container and click Edit Rule .

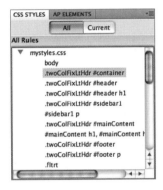

4 When the "CSS Rule Definition for .twoColFixLtI Idr #container in mystyles.css" dialog box opens, click Background in the Category column.

5 Click Browse and, in the Select Image Source dialog box, navigate to the images folder. Select line.gif.

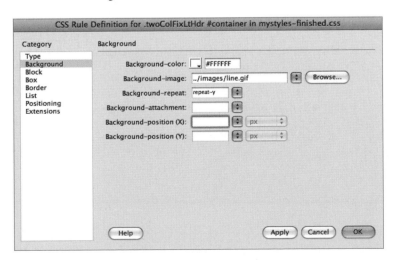

Note: If you look at line.gif in Photoshop or Fireworks, you'll find a graphic the exact width of the container with a line meant to repeat down the page.

6 From the Background-repeat pop-up menu, choose repeat-y. Click OK.

This will repeat the image on the y-axis down the length of the container element.

7 Choose File > Save All.

Because the CSS style rule is stored in an external style sheet, Dreamweaver automatically changes the file to change the style. Both the main document and the style sheet

Naxos is a large island with charming seaside villages, mountain villages, hiking trails, and wonderful fresh seafood.

must be saved to store the current document look and feel. Immediately above the Document window, you see buttons representing Source Code and any linked files, such as mystyles.css. An unsaved file is marked with an asterisk (*). Choosing File > Save All will save the HTML file and any linked files that may have been changed.

Using the Properties panel with images

The optimum web graphic usage balances image dimensions and quality with file size. Web designers frequently need to optimize graphics that already have been placed on the page. Dreamweaver includes a graphics engine that is perfect for realizing the clearest image at the smallest possible file size. In this exercise, you'll use Dreamweaver tools to optimize and rescale an image for the web, a common design-time task.

1 If necessary, open the naxos.html file by double-clicking its entry in the Files panel.

2 If necessary, choose Window > Properties to display the Properties panel.

Select an image in the Document window. When an image is selected in the document, a number of options for image editing appear in the Properties panel under the Alt field. See the sidebar "Dreamweaver's graphic tools" for an explanation of each button.

In the Properties panel, you can click the image button to edit it in Photoshop or Fireworks. The other buttons allow you to edit the image's settings in the Dreamweaver image preview dialog where you can crop, or adjust contrast and sharpness.

3   With the image selected in the Properties panel, click the Edit Image Settings button ![Ps]. When the Image Preview dialog box opens, verify that JPEG is chosen in the Format list. Drag the Quality slider to 79.

The Image Preview dialog box includes many image-optimization options, including the ability to switch from one web graphic format to another, such as converting a GIF image to JPEG. Using the JPEG format, you can also control the degree of quality: the higher the quality, the more detailed the image appearance but the larger its file size. Let's use the comparison feature to strike the optimal balance between clarity and size.

4   In the lower right of the Image Preview dialog box, click the 2-up button ![2up]. When the preview splits into two views, click the bottom view and drag the Quality slider to 40.

▶ **Tip:** In Dreamweaver Preferences for File Types/Editors, you can set up Fireworks, Photoshop, or any other image editor as your primary choice. When you have done this, clicking the Edit button on the Properties panel will open the file in your image editor of choice. If you have not set the Preferences for an image editor, clicking the Edit button in the image tools opens a dialog box asking you to select your preferred image editor. Clicking another image editing button, such as Edit Image Settings, will open the image in the Dreamweaver Image Preview dialog.

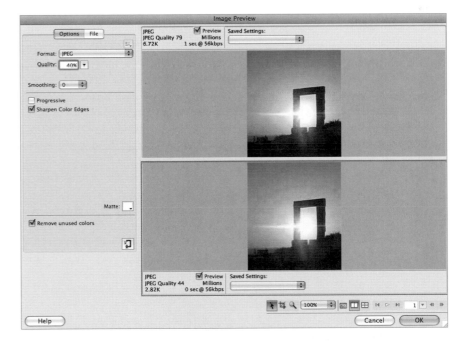

As you can see, the image quality between the two previews is noticeably different. The file-size differences—6.72K for the JPEG at 79 and 2.82K for the image at 40—are not very significant and don't fully compensate for the loss in quality. At 40, the image quality has degraded visibly. Leave the image quality at 79% by selecting the top window and clicking OK.

5   Choose File > Save to store your work.

Dreamweaver's graphic tools

All of Dreamweaver's graphic tools are accessible from the Properties panel when an image is selected. These are the six tools:

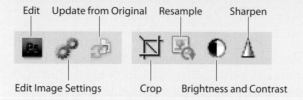

- Edit—Sends the selected image to the defined external graphic editor. You can assign a graphics editing program to any given file type in the File Types/Editors category of the Preferences dialog box. The tool button image changes according to the program chosen. For example, if Fireworks is the designated editor for the image type, a Fireworks icon is shown; if Photoshop is the editor, you'll see a Photoshop icon.

- Edit Image Settings—Opens the current image in the Image Preview dialog box. In addition to providing access to the optimization features used in this exercise, the Image Preview dialog box can be used to crop images and modify animated GIF settings.

- Update from Original—Renders a Smart Object to the newly selected size. The underlying Photoshop file is unchanged.

- Crop—Removes the unwanted parts of an image. When the Crop tool is selected, a bounding box with a series of handles appears within the current image. You can adjust the bounding box size by dragging the handles. When the box outlines the desired portion of the image, double-click the graphic to remove those parts of the image that are outside the bounding box.

- Resample—Rescales a resized image. The Resample tool is active only when an image has been resized.

- Brightness and Contrast—Adjusts an image that may be too light or too dark. A dialog presents two sliders—for brightness and contrast—that can be adjusted independently. A live preview is available so that you can evaluate adjustments before committing to them.

- Sharpen—Affects the definition of image edges by raising or lowering the contrast of pixels on a scale from 0 to 10. As with the Brightness and Contrast tool, Sharpen offers a real-time preview.

You can undo all graphic operations by choosing Edit > Undo until the containing document is closed or you quit Dreamweaver.

Copying and pasting from Photoshop

Many Web designers use Photoshop to initially compose (or "comp") their site layouts. To create the final Dreamweaver layout, only portions of those Photoshop graphics are needed, because other page elements are text- or CSS-based. When using Photoshop CS4 and Dreamweaver CS4, it's easy to copy any needed selection from the graphic comp in Photoshop and paste it into the Dreamweaver layout. The Image Preview dialog box acts as the intermediary to convert the file to the necessary format.

● **Note:** The following exercise requires Adobe Photoshop CS4.

1   If necessary, open the naxos.html file by double-clicking its entry in the Files panel.

2   Place your mouse pointer after the paragraph *The mountains shelter golden fertile valleys where you'll see fields and crops mingled with small churches and imposing churches.* A blank paragraph marks the location.

3   Open Photoshop CS4 and choose File > Open. When the Open dialog box appears, open images > PSD >naxos-images.psd. Click Open.

    The file contains layers; each image is on a separate layer.

4   If necessary, choose Window > Layers to bring the Layers panel to the top. In the Layers panel, select the Happy Family layer.

5   In the Tools palette, choose the Rectangular Marquee tool and drag a selection around the image of the happy family.

6   Choose Edit > Copy. Close Photoshop without saving the image and return to Dreamweaver.

7   In Dreamweaver, choose Edit > Paste. When the Image Preview dialog box opens, verify that JPEG – Better Quality is chosen in the Saved Settings pop-up menu, and click OK.

● **Note:** If you wanted your selection to include elements on more than one layer, choose Edit > Copy Merged.

Note: This image is used on the naxos-finished.html page and already exists in the images folder. Click Replace to replace it with the image you are now saving

8   When the Save Web Image dialog box opens, navigate to the images folder. In the "File name" field, type **happy-family.jpg**, and click Save.

The image copied from Photoshop is inserted into the document.

9   Choose File > Save.

Although Dreamweaver will connect this image to the original Photoshop file, it is not "smart" like an Adobe Photoshop Smart Object, because it cannot be used on different pages in different sizes. You will work with a Smart Object later in the lesson.

Accessing Adobe Bridge

Adobe Bridge CS4 is an aptly named program that acts as a bridge between Adobe Creative Suite applications, including Dreamweaver. Using Bridge, you can quickly browse directories of images and other supported assets, tag files with keywords, and easily access professional stock-images sites, such as Adobe Stock Photos. Bridge is fully integrated with Dreamweaver: You can launch Bridge from within Dreamweaver, drag images from Bridge into Dreamweaver, and you can do it all without ever leaving Bridge.

1 If necessary, open the naxos.html file by double-clicking its entry in the Files panel.

2 Place your mouse pointer at the beginning of the content area, under the heading *The essential Greek isle*.

3 Choose File > Browse in Bridge. A dialog box will ask you if you always want to open Bridge at login. Because you won't use Bridge in future exercises, you can click No.

4 When Bridge opens, click the Folders tab and navigate to the images > BridgeSource folder.

5 Choose View > Compact Mode. Alternatively, you could click Switch to Compact Mode (the last button to the right of the top row of controls).

Using Compact mode reduces the size of the Bridge interface to about one-fourth of the screen and, by default, always keeps the program on top of others for easy browsing and dragging.

6 If necessary, drag the slider to reduce image previews to a smaller size. Drag the entire window as needed to position it so that you can see the images both in Bridge and in the Dreamweaver document.

7 Drag girl-on-beach.jpg from Bridge into Dreamweaver and place it at the beginning of the content.

8 In the Image Tag Accessibility Attributes dialog box, type **Getting some sun**. Click OK.

9 In Dreamweaver, choose File > Save. Click Live View, or press F12 (Windows) or Option+F12 (Mac), to preview the page in your primary browser. When you're done, return to Bridge and close the program.

The essential Greek isle

Using Photoshop Smart Objects

Unlike other images, Smart Objects have a connection to a Photoshop (PSD) file. If a PSD file is altered in any manner, Dreamweaver recognizes those changes and offers to update the web image. A single PSD file can be placed in multiple pages as a Photoshop Smart Object, and all the appearances of the image can be updated in one action.

1 If necessary, open naxos.html.

2 In the sidebar, double-click the church image placeholder.

3 In the Select Image Source dialog box, browse to images > PSD > naxos-church. psd. Click OK (Windows) or Choose (Mac).

Alternatively, you could drag a PSD image from the Assets panel to Dreamweaver. In either case, the Image Preview dialog box will open.

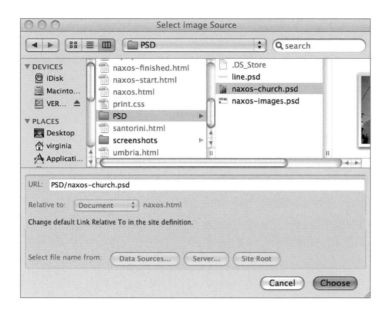

4 In the Image Preview dialog box, from the Format pop-up menu, choose JPEG. Leave the Quality field at 80%. Click OK.

▶ **Tip:** In a JPEG image, quality is expressed in percentages, ranging from 0 to 100%. An image may appear for the first time at a particular percentage based on the source of the image—perhaps a digital camera. On the other hand, in a GIF image, quality is expressed by the number of colors. More colors mean a larger GIF file size, but not necessarily higher quality. Some GIF images contain a limited number of colors and can remain at high quality, even when the number of colors is reduced to lower the file size.

5 In the Save Web Image dialog box, navigate to images and click Save As to save the file as **naxos-church.jpg**. This image is used on the naxosfinished.html page and already exists in the images folder. Click Replace to replace it with the one you are saving now.

6 In the Image Tag Accessibility Attributes dialog box, type **A Naxos church**. Click OK. If the "Image Tag Accessibility Attributes" dialog box does not appear, type the phrase in the Alt field on the Properties panel.

You see a Smart Object badge in the upper-left corner. It indicates that this image is "in sync" with the original PSD file with a green circular arrow. However, with a width of 300 pixels, the image is too large for the sidebar.

7 At the lower right of the image, Shift-drag the resize handle upward and inward to resize the image. Holding down Shift while resizing retains the image's original proportions. Watch the Width measurement in the Properties panel and stop when you reach 200px.

The Smart Object badge in the upper-left corner indicates that the image is now out of sync. Place the mouse pointer over the Smart Object badge, and you are informed that the dimensions of the web image are different from the selected HTML width and height.

8 Right-click (Windows) or Control-click (Mac) the image and, from the context menu, select Update from Original.

The updated Smart Object is sized and resampled for this instance. However, the underlying Photoshop file remains in its original state for use in other places as a Smart Object and could be optimized to other sizes in other locations. If the PSD file were changed in any way, all instances of Smart Objects tied to the file would update immediately.

To use the same PSD file in another page, insert the image on that page using the same steps you just completed. You would have two images linked to the same PSD source file. The new image might be quite different in size, perhaps just a thumbnail, but both images will link to the same PSD image.

In this lesson, you learned how you can use Dreamweaver to insert foreground and background images into a page, you added Image placeholders, and replaced those placeholders with actual images. You also browsed images in Adobe Bridge and dragged images from Bridge into Dreamweaver. You used the Properties panel to preview and edit images. If you own Photoshop, you were able to copy a layer in a Photoshop file and paste it into Dreamweaver. Finally, you took a Photoshop file (a PSD document) and created a Photoshop Smart Object in Dreamweaver that can be used multiple times.

● **Note:** If the image had been scaled larger and beyond the limits of quality allowed in the PSD file, you would see a warning that the chosen image size exceeded that of the original PSD file. You could right-click (Windows) or Control-click (Mac) and select Reset Size to Original To return to 100% of the underlying PSD file.

Review questions

1 Describe at least two methods for inserting an image into a web page using Dreamweaver.

2 What is the purpose of using an image placeholder?

3 How do you insert a background image? What control do you have over background graphics?

4 True or false: All graphics have to be optimized outside of Dreamweaver.

5 What is the advantage of using a Photoshop Smart Object over copying and pasting an image from Photoshop?

Review answers

1 One method is to choose Image from the Common category of the Insert panel and navigate to the graphic file you want to insert. Another method is to drag the graphic file from the Assets panel onto a web page. Images also can be copied and pasted from Photoshop. Finally, images can be found and inserted in a web page by browsing in Adobe Bridge.

2 Image placeholders are a design-time tool. They are an aid to planning a layout before final images are available. Browsers either completely omit the image placeholder or indicate that the image is not found.

3 CSS style rules are used to add a background image to a page element. Choose the selector of the element that will contain the background image, such as the <body> tag or a specific ID applied to a <div> tag, and then add the appropriate background image properties. Background images, by default, tile to fill the containing space; but using CSS, you can display the image only once, or tile on either an x- or y-axis.

4 False. Any image inserted into a Dreamweaver page can be optimized within the Image Preview dialog box. Optimization can include rescaling, changing format, or fine-tuning of format settings.

5 A Smart Object can be used multiple times in different places on a site. Each instance of the Smart Object can be assigned individual settings, yet remain connected to the original image. If the original image is updated, all the connected images are immediately updated, as well. When copying all or part of a Photoshop file to paste into Dreamweaver, you get a single image that can have only one set of values applied to it.

5 WORKING WITH NAVIGATION

In this lesson, you'll apply several kinds of links to page elements by doing the following:

- Apply a text link to a page within the same site.

- Create a navigation bar

- Create tabbed panels

- Create a link using an image

- Create a link to a page on another website

- Establish an e-mail link

 This lesson will take about 60 minutes to complete. Be sure you have copied Lessons > lesson05 and Lessons > SpryAssets from the *Adobe Dreamweaver CS4 Classroom in a Book* CD onto your hard drive before beginning. If you already have a SpryAssets folder in your CIB folder, replace it with the one from the CD.

About Here and Back Travel

- Home
- Italy ▶
- Greece ▶
- About Us ▶

Meet our friendly staff

When you call our office in New York City, you will be connected to one of our experienced, helpful and friendly staff members. This is Here and Back Travel. Find our <u>office location</u>.

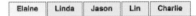

| Elaine | Linda | Jason | Lin | Charlie |

ELAINE is the President and CEO of Here and Back Travel. She has 20 years experience in the travel industry and has traveled extensively to research the hotels and restaurants we recommend.

You may find her answering your phone calls or checking out a recommended hotel on Santorini.

<u>Email Elaine</u>.

Dreamweaver handles many variations of links ranging from hyperlinks to e-mail links and does so with ease and flexibility.

Previewing your completed file

To see the final version of the file you will work on in the first part of this lesson, let's preview the completed page in the browser.

1   Open Adobe Dreamweaver CS4.

2   If necessary, press F8 to open the Files panel, and choose DW CIB from the site list.

3   In the Files panel, expand the lesson05 folder.

4   Select the about-finished.html file, and press F12 (Windows) or Option+F12 (Mac).

5   When the page opens in your primary browser, click Greece in the navigation bar in the sidebar. When the pop-up menu opens, click Santorini. Click the browser's Back button to return to about-finished.html. Click the names in the tabbed panels to see the information about the people. If you have a mail client installed on your system, click one of the e-mail links for the individual workers. When the e-mail message window opens, close it.

    The page includes links to pages within the same site, as well as external and e-mail links.

6   Close your browser and return to Dreamweaver.

Linking to internal site pages

Links are a quintessential element of the web, and Dreamweaver makes it easy to apply them. Links add the *hyper* in hypertext and are the engine that moves website users from one location to another. In this exercise, you'll create a text link to a page in the same site through a variety of methods.

1   In the Files panel, expand the lesson05 folder and double-click the about-start.html file to open it.

2   Choose File > Save As. Save the file as *about.html* in the lesson05 folder on your hard drive. If you need to open the unaltered about-start.html page again, it will be preserved on your hard drive.

3 Select the text that reads *Contact Us*.

4 If necessary, choose Window > Properties to open the Properties panel. When you create links, make sure that the HTML tab is selected in the Properties panel. Click Browse for File 📁, the folder icon adjacent to the Link field. When the Select File dialog box opens, navigate to the lesson05 folder and select contact.html. Make sure that the "Relative to" pop-up menu is set to Document. Click Choose.

● **Note:** Some web servers can work with links that are relative to the site root, rather than to the document. Unless you are sure your server works with root-relative links, choose Document.

5 Click anywhere in the Document window to deselect the link text for a clearer view.

The default formatting for a link is blue text with a blue underline. Therefore, the new link you created is blue text on a blue background. You can change that to improve readability.

6 In the tag selector, select the <a> and click the New CSS Rule icon in the CSS Style panel. A link is created with an <a> tag, the anchor element.

Dreamweaver suggests a Compound selector.

7 Click Less Specific until the selector is "#footer p a."

8 In the "CSS Rule Definition for #footer p a in mystyles.css" dialog box, select the Type category, and use the color picker to select the color white, #FFF. Click OK.

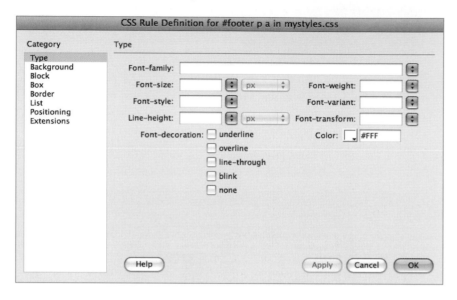

The link text is now white. Any <a> tag that appears in the footer will use this style rule and display as white text with a white underline.

The Browse for Folder method is one technique for linking to files. Next, let's try a more visual approach.

9 If necessary, press F8 to open the Files panel, and expand the lesson05 folder. Double-click the file santorini.html to open it. Find the *Contact Us* text in the footer and select it.

You can select any range of text to create a link; Dreamweaver will add the necessary tags around the selected text.

10 In the Properties panel, drag the Point to File icon ⊕—the target icon next to the Link field—to contact.html in the Local Files panel.

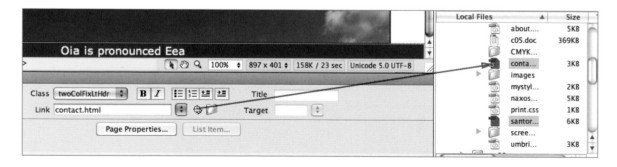

11 If a folder in the Files panel contains a page you want to link to but the folder is not open, drag the Point to File icon over the folder and hold it in place to expand that folder so that you can point to the desired file.

Because the file santorini.html is linked to mystyles.css, the link will automatically display in the white color you added to the style sheet for links in the footer area.

12 Choose File > Save All.

13 Close santorini.html. Leave about.html open for the next exercise.

You learned two methods for creating hyperlinks with the Properties panel. You used the Browse button to find the file you want to link to. And you learned how to use Point to File. Either linking technique can create a graphic-based link.

Creating an external link

The pages you linked in the previous exercise were within the current site. You can also link to any page on the web, if you know the full web address, or URL. You can link an image to an internal site page or to an external site. In this exercise, you'll use an image to create an external link and create a matching text link.

1 If necessary, open the about.html file that you worked on in the previous exercise by double-clicking its entry in the Files panel.

2 In the sidebar, select the image of New York City.

3 In the Properties panel, type **http://maps.google.com/maps** and press Enter (or Return).

4 Choose File > Save, and use Live view or press F12 (Windows) or Option+F12 (Mac) to preview the page. Note that when your mouse pointer hovers over the image, it changes to a hand to indicate a link. If you click the image, the browser will take you to the opening page of Google Maps, assuming you have a connection to the Internet. Click Live View again, or close your browser and return to Dreamweaver.

5 To create the same link as text, position your mouse pointer at the end of the opening paragraph on the page, after *This is Here and Back Travel.* Type **Find our office location**.

● **Note:** If the web address is too long or complex to type, browse to the desired page in your browser, and copy the URL from the location field. Then paste it into the Link field in Dreamweaver's Properties panel.

● **Note:** Just as links are underlined by default, images used as links are given a border by default. To prevent the linked image from displaying a border, the mystyles.css contains a new rule: .twoColFixLtHdr #sidebar1 a img {border: 0;}.

6 Select the words *office location*. In the Properties panel Link field, type **http://maps.google.com/maps**, and press Enter (or Return).

7 Choose File > Save.

It is just that easy to create links to internal site pages or external URLs using either text or images in Dreamweaver.

Setting up e-mail links

Another popular type of link is the e-mail link that can create an automatic, pre-addressed e-mail message for your visitors, which is useful for receiving customer feedback, product orders, or other important communications. The code is different from the standard page link. Dreamweaver can automatically create the proper code for any e-mail link.

1 If necessary, open the about.html file that you worked on in the previous exercise by double-clicking its entry in the Files panel.

2 Place your mouse pointer at the end of the text *about Elaine* and press Return (or Enter) to create a new paragraph. Type **Email Elaine.**

3 Select the words *Email Elaine*.

4 In the Common category of the Insert panel, click Email Link , the envelope icon.

5 When the Email Link dialog box appears, notice that Dreamweaver entered the selected text into the Text field of the dialog box. Leave the current entry in the Text field unchanged and, in the E-Mail field, type **elaine@fakeaddress.com**. Click OK.

There's no need to type the *mailto:* preface; Dreamweaver handles the coding automatically, as you see in the link field in the Properties panel

6 Choose File > Save. If you have an e-mail program installed on your computer, use Live view or press F12 to preview the page, and click the just-applied e-mail link. After the e-mail message appears, notice that the To field is already addressed to the fake e-mail address for Elaine.

7 Close both the message and your browser, or click Live View to return to Dreamweaver.

The function of the type of link depends on the client e-mail program installed on the user's computer, such as Outlook, Entourage, or Apple Mail. The link will not work, however, if a user sends her mail via an Internet application, such as Hotmail or Gmail. If you want to increase the odds that you'll get e-mail from as many of your web visitors as possible, you can use a form to collect comments and feedback from your site visitors (see Lesson 8, "Working with Forms," to learn more about creating forms).

Targeting links within a page

Typically, when you click a link to a page, the browser window displays the page from the top down. Certain designs, such as very long pages, require an approach that allows linking to a specific point anywhere on the page. You can insert a link anywhere on the page and link directly to any element with an ID on the same page. In this exercise, you'll take advantage of an ID you created earlier in the table element so you can link to a specific section near the bottom of the page.

1 Reopen the santorini.html file by double-clicking its entry in the Files panel.

   Let's start by adding some new text for our link.

2 Click your mouse pointer in the sidebar after the text *fun-filled sunshine* and press Enter (Windows) or Return (Mac) to create a new paragraph.

3 Type **Check our recommended hotels**.

4 Select the words *recommended hotels*. In the Properties panel, in the Link field, type **#hotels** and press Return (or Enter).

> *Santorini is perfect for beautiful oceans and fun-filled sunshine.*
>
> Check our <u>recommended hotels</u>.

You have created a link to the location on the page where the table with the ID hotels is placed.

The hash mark, or number sign, #, designates a link to a specific ID on this page. The word following the hash mark—*hotels*, in this example—is the name of the ID. This ID was already on the page. If you have a lengthy page that needs links of this type, you can add unique IDs to headings, lists, paragraphs, or other items on the page to create targets for your links. To create a link to the recommended hotels table from another page in the site, the link would include both the filename and the ID name, like this: santorini.html#hotels.

5   Choose File > Save. Use Live view or your browser to test the link. Then return to Dreamweaver Edit mode.

6   Close santorini.html. Leave about.html open for the next exercise.

Learning about Ajax and Spry

Leading web designers touted the arrival of Web 2.0 as a new era in Internet usability and interactivity. The prime technology driving Web 2.0 is known as Ajax, an acronym for Asynchronous JavaScript and XML. If you've ever scrolled through a Google Map or browsed a photo collection on Flickr, you've experienced what Ajax can do.

The key term in the Ajax acronym is *asynchronous*, which literally means "not at the same time." Normally, viewing pages on the web is a very linear process. For example, let's say you're reviewing information on a company site. Here's what happens in a standard website:

1   You visit a page with your browser.

2   The initial page is sent from a remote web server.

3   Your browser renders the page.

4   You click a link on the page to learn more.

5   Your browser requests a new page with additional information from the remote web server.

6   The web server sends the new page.

7   Your browser loads the page and displays it as an entirely new page.

Here's how the same operation works with an Ajax-driven page:

1   You visit a page with your browser.

2   The initial page is sent from a remote web server.

3   Your browser renders the page and, simultaneously, loads all related data into the Ajax engine.

4   You click a link on the page to learn more.

5   Acting like a middleman, the Ajax engine intercepts the new request and returns any relevant details.

6   Your browser displays the new details on the existing page and updates only the relevant section of the page.

Essentially, Ajax loads relevant data for a page but does not display it until requested. This makes the user experience much smoother and more interactive. Should more data be required than was initially loaded, the Ajax engine downloads the data from the web server in the background and then delivers it to the browser for display only as it is needed.

Most implementations of Ajax require an advanced knowledge of JavaScript and a great deal of hand coding. To ease the learning curve, Adobe has developed an Ajax framework known as Spry that integrates seamlessly with Dreamweaver CS4. There are four sets of Spry tools:

- Spry Data – Incorporates HTML or XML data into any web page and allows for the Ajax-style interactive display of data. You will work with a Spry Data set in Lesson 6.

- Spry Form widgets – Combines form elements, such as text fields and lists, with JavaScript validation functions and user-friendly error messages. You will work with Spry Form widgets in Lesson 8.

- Spry Layout widgets – Provides a series of sophisticated layout controls, including tabbed and Accordion Panels. You work with Spry Tabbed Panels and menu bars later in this lesson. In Lesson 6, you will work with Spry Accordion Panels.

- Spry Effects – Extends the Dreamweaver behavior library with advanced functionality to interactively affect page elements. Spry effects include the ability to fade, reveal, slide, highlight, and shake targeted page components.

If you'd like to peek under the hood and learn more about how Spry works, visit Adobe Labs at http://labs.adobe.com/technologies/spry/.

Inserting Spry Menu Bars

Every website needs internal navigation. Most websites designed in the last few years use site navigation and menu bars based on CSS-styled lists. With a bit of added JavaScript, the list can become a compact vertical or horizontal menu with subcategories that pop up. Dreamweaver Spry Menu Bars are an easy and powerful way to insert all the needed HTML list and link code, all the CSS rules that will make them appear as menu bars, and all the JavaScript to make the subcategories pop up.

Spry Menu Bars have the advantage of being nothing more than lists in the underlying HTML, so even if a website user doesn't have JavaScript or CSS enabled, the menu bar still functions as a set of workable navigation links.

1 If necessary, double-click the about.html file to open it in Dreamweaver.

2 In the sidebar, select the image of New York City. Press the Left Arrow key to move the selection off the image and establish an insertion point to the left of the image. Then press Return (or Enter) to create an empty space before the image. Click in the empty line.

3 In the Spry category of the Insert panel, click the Spry Menu Bar icon.

4 In the Spry Menu Bar dialog box, select Vertical, and click OK.

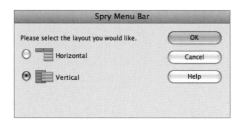

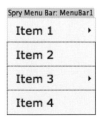

5 The menu bar will appear on your page. To select the menu bar in the document, click in the blue bar at the top.

6 Before customizing the menu bar, choose File > Save. If Dreamweaver asks you about copying dependent files, click OK.

With the menu bar selected, the Properties panel is used to create the links.

Dreamweaver inserts a folder called SpryAssets into your CIB Lessons site root folder to work any Spry widget. The CSS and JavaScript files needed for the menu bar are added to this folder. To preview the finished page, you already added this folder to your hard drive. Some of the necessary files are already located in the SpryAssets folder and will be attached to your HTML page at this time.

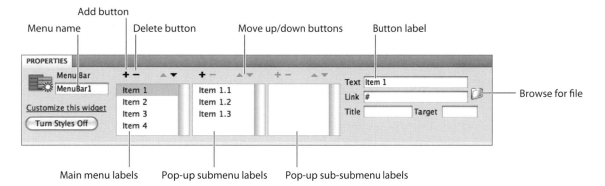

7 Highlight Item 1 in the Main menu labels window. Then, in the Item 1 Text field, replace the Untitled Item text by typing **Home**, and in the Link field delete the # and type **index.html**. Delete Item 1.1, Item 1.2, and Item 1.3 by clicking the minus icon above the pop-up submenu labels column.

8 Highlight Item 2 in the Main menu lables window, then in the Item 2 Text field, type **Italy**. Leave the hash mark in the Link field. In the pop-up submenu column, click the Plus button to add an item. In the Untitled Item field, type **Umbria**, and in the Link field, replace the hash mark by typing **umbria.html**.

9 Select Item 3. Replace the text in the Text field with **Greece**. Leave the Link field as it is. Select Item 3.1. Replace the text in the Text field with **Santorini**, and type **santorini.html** in the Link field to replace the hash mark.

10 Select Item 3.2. Replace the text by typing **Naxos**, and type **naxos.html** in the Link field to replace the hash mark. Delete Item 3.3 by selecting it and clicking the minus sign above the column.

11 Select Item 4. In the Text field, type **About Us**. In the Link field, type **about.html**.

● **Note:** The hash mark (#), while not a link to any page in your site, creates a trigger that simulates a link and allows the pop-up submenu to open. Without either a hash mark or a real link in the main menu Link field, the pop-up submenu would not appear.

12 Click the Plus button above the pop-up submenu labels window to create Item 4.1. Select Item 4.1. In the Text field, type **Contact Us**. In the Link field, type **contact.html**.

13 Choose File > Save. The completed links appear in the Document window.

Clicking one of the unselected main nav labels in the left column of the Properties panel should make any pop-up menus disappear in the Document window.

14 In the Properties panel, click Turn Styles Off. In the document, you see the unstyled list you just created using the Properties panel.

You may find it easier to work in the Document window instead of in the Properties panel. By clicking Turn Styles Off, you can use the unstyled nested lists in the Document window to type text and create links in the lists that generate the HTML code for the menu bar.

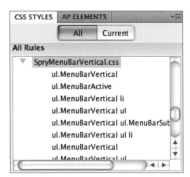

15 In the Properties panel, click Turn Styles On to return to the styled appearance.

● **Note:** Not all browsing devices use CSS. For example, some of the less-capable mobile devices do not. Your menu will display as a list on those devices, but the links will still be completely usable.

16 Choose File > Save All. Dreamweaver will save the dependent CSS and JavaScript files in the SpryAssets folder.

17 Use Live view or your browser to preview the page and test your new menu bar. Since none of the other pages have a menu bar yet, click the Back button to return to about.html. Click Live View or close your browser to return to Edit mode.

You'll learn about Dreamweaver templates, Library items, and server-side includes in Lesson 10, which will give you several easily maintained ways to add the new menu bar to every page in your site.

Customizing the appearance of the Spry Menu Bar

The Spry Menu Bar offers a way to create a professional-looking menu quickly and easily. Styling it is just as easy. Its default color choices could use a tune-up to work better with the site color scheme. You saw earlier that Dreamweaver added some CSS and JavaScript files to your site. You may also have noticed that a file called SpryMenuBarVertical.css was linked to your page.

1 In the CSS Styles panel, scroll through the styles until you find SpryMenuBarVertical.css and then expand it. Be careful not to select SpryMenuBarVertical-finished.css. Although it should not be linked to this page, it is included in the SpryAssets folder so you can preview the finished page.

2 In the All Rules pane, select the style `ul.MenuBarVertical a`. This rule affects the color and background color of the links, or the <a> elements. If necessary, drag the lower edge of the CSS Styles panel downward to reveal the Properties pane. In the Properties pane, click the background-color color box and use the color picker to select #FF0, a bright yellow. Then, click the color box and use the color picker to select #00C, a dark blue. Press Return (Windows) or Enter (Mac).

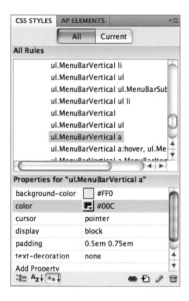

3 In the All Rules pane, select the `ul.MenuBarVertical ul li` style. This rule affects the width of the submenu items. In the Properties pane, change the width from 8.3 em to 200px. Since the sidebar is a fixed width, the width of the menu bar should be constrained as well.

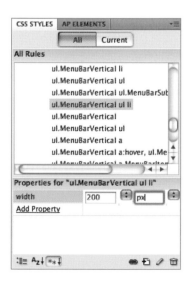

4 In the All Rules pane, select the ul.MenuBarVertical li" rule. This controls the main menu list, but it needs a couple of changes. Click the Edit Rule icon (which looks like a pencil) to edit this style in the "CSS Rule Definition for ul.MenuBarVertical li in SpryMenuBarVertical.css" dialog box.

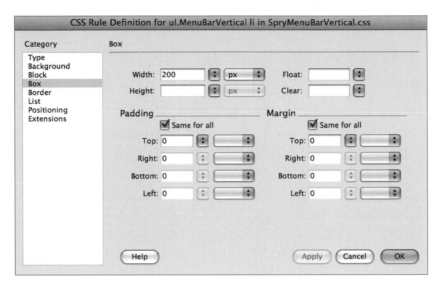

5 Select the Box category and, in the Width field, type **200**.

6 Select the Border category. Deselect the "Same for all" check boxes for Style, Width, and Color. In the Right and Bottom fields, type **solid** in the Style column, in the Width column type **1** and choose **px**, and in the Color column type **#00C.** Click OK.

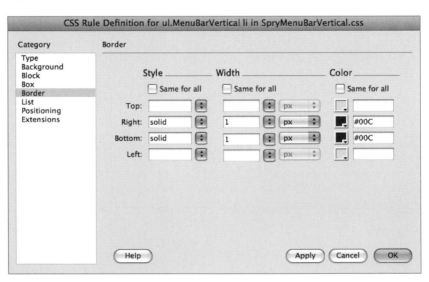

7 Choose File > Save All.

8 Use Live View or your browser to examine the appearance of the menu bar.

9 Click Live View again or close your browser to return to Dreamweaver's Edit mode.

● **Note:** To change the positioning of the pop-up submenu, edit the `ul.MenuBarVertical ul` style for margin. You can use background images instead of colors by editing the styles for various `<a>` rules, including `ul.MenuBarVertical a.MenuBarItemHover`.

A horizontal Spry Menu Bar is inserted in the same way. One big difference in styling a horizontal menu bar is that the width of the buttons on a horizontal menu bar is determined by the number of buttons in the menu. For example, a horizontal menu bar with five buttons would be wider than a horizontal menu bar with four buttons.

Inserting Spry Tabbed Panels

Spry Tabbed Panels are designed to help users navigate a single page without scrolling by organizing content into a series of tabbed panels. A Spry Tabbed Panel can be placed anywhere in a web page, provided that you have enough horizontal space to accommodate the tabs. In this exercise, you will organize the personal profiles on the about.html page into Spry Tabbed Panels.

1 If necessary, open about.html from the lesson05 folder by double-clicking the filename in the Files panel.

2 Click after the opening paragraph of the page to insert the cursor, then press Return (or Enter) to create a new paragraph. Leave your mouse pointer in that location as the insertion point for the Spry Tabbed Panel.

3 In the Spry category of the Insert panel, click the Spry Tabbed Panel icon.

The Spry Tabbed Panel appears on the page. Don't worry if the Spry element pushes Elaine's <div> off to the right; when you're finished, everything will look fine.

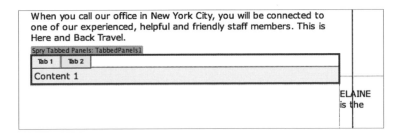

● **Note:** The customized CSS rules for the SpryTabbedPanels.css were already present in the SpryAssets folder that you copied to your hard drive from the CD. The changes will be explained at the end of the exercise. The colors you will see are not the colors that normally appear by default with Spry Tabbed Panels.

The Spry Tabbed Panel has two parts: the labeled tab and a content area for each tab. You can place any content in the content area: text, graphics, tables, lists, forms, or even Flash movies.

4 Use the Properties panel to add three more panels. Five are needed on this page. Click the Panels Plus (+) button three times.

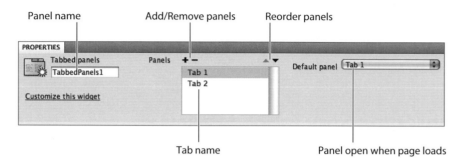

In the Document window, Dreamweaver displays an eye icon to allow you to select a currently hidden panel's content and make the contents ready to edit.

5 Select the text in Tab 1 and type **Elaine.**

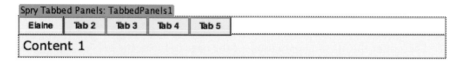

6 Drag your mouse pointer in the Content 1 area to delete the text *Content 1.*

7 Place your mouse pointer anywhere within the profile for Elaine. It's off to the side, but you can still click in it. Then choose <div.profile> in the tag selector to select the entire <div>.

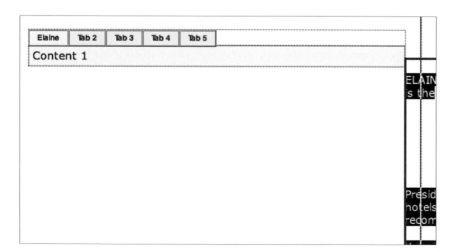

8 Choose Edit > Cut, or press Control+X (Windows) or Command+X (Mac).

9 Move your mouse pointer back into the empty area for Content 1. Choose Edit > Paste, or press Control+V (Windows) or Command+V (Mac).

The <div.profile> about Elaine now appears as the content for the first tab. Because the information about Elaine was cut from its former position, the profile for Linda has been moved up and pushed off to the side.

10 Repeat steps 5 to 9 to change the tab names to Linda, Jason, Lin, and Charlie, and to cut and paste each person's <div.profile> into the content area for their respective tabs. You can choose the eye icon to move around and check the content for each tab when you've finished. Should you want to edit or add more content, find the appropriate content pane using the eye icon.

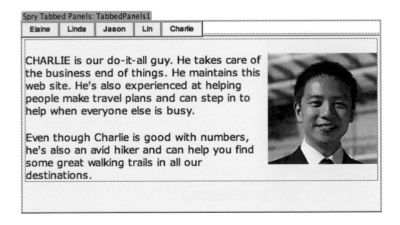

11 Choose File > Save All.

12 Use Live view or your browser to preview the page and try out the new tabbed panels. When you're finished, click Live View again or close your browser to return to Dreamweaver.

Notice that when the page first renders in Live view or the browser, Tab 1 opens by default.

Spry Tabbed Panels are technically not navigation. They don't move a user from page to page or to selected targets on a page. However, they do provide a way to "navigate" a variety of content on a particular topic by organizing it into clickable, tabbed panels that concentrate content into a smaller block and eliminate scrolling.

The CSS rules that were changed in SpryTabbedPanels.css to customize this widget's colors are .TabbedPanelsTab, .TabbedPanelsTabHover, .TabbedPanelsTabSelected, and .TabbedPanelsContentGroup.

Checking your page

Dreamweaver will automatically check your page for browser compatibility, accessibility, and broken links. In this exercise, you'll check your links and learn what you can do in case of a browser compatibility problem.

1 If necessary, open about.html from the lesson05 folder in the Files panel.

2 Choose File > Check Page > Links.

A Link Checker panel opens. The Link Checker panel reports that there is a broken link to index.html. You'll make this page in Lesson 9, so there's no need to worry about fixing this broken link now. The Link Checker will also find broken links to external sites, should you have any.

3 Double-click the Link Checker tab to close the panel.

4 Choose File > Check Page > Browser Compatibility.

The Browser Compatibility report opens.

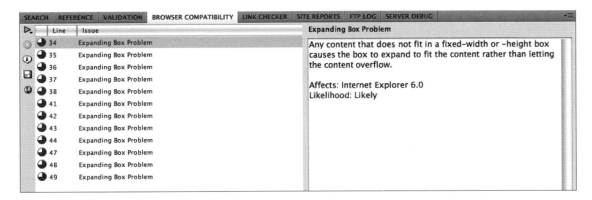

A number of browser compatibility problems are identified, but it's actually just a single problem that is occurring in several places—you can see specific line numbers in the code where the problem can be found. Luckily, Adobe.com is prepared to help you solve problems using a Page Check operation.

5 Select a problem name—since they are all the same Expanding Box Problem, any one will do.

6 With a problem name selected, click the small More Info icon ⓘ in the first column on the left side of the report.

A web page at Adobe.com opens. In that page, the problem is explained and a solution is offered that you can implement on your Dreamweaver page. Some suggested fixes are meant for particular browsers or devices that you may not want to support. In these cases, you can ignore the suggestions. Since this page will not be published to the Internet, we will ignore them entirely."

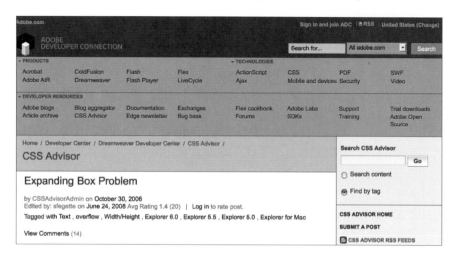

● **Note:** You can also check your page for several other problems using the Site > Reports menu. These reports are helpful because they point out issues like missing page titles and missing alt text that you may have overlooked.

7 Close the browser and return to Dreamweaver.

8 Double-click the Browser Compatibility tab to close it.

You've made big changes to the appearance of the pages in this lesson by adding a menu bar and by creating links to specific positions on a page, to e-mail, and to an external site. You also created a link that uses an image as the clickable item and reorganized a page's content into Spry Tabbed Panels. Finally, you checked your page for broken links and browser compatibility.

Review questions

1 Describe two ways to insert a link into a page.

2 What information is required to create a link to an external web page?

3 What's the difference between standard page links and e-mail links?

4 What are the benefits of using Spry Menu Bars?

5 What are the advantages of using Spry Tabbed Panels?

Review answers

1 Select text or a graphic; then, in the Properties panel, select the Browse for File icon next to the Link field and navigate to the desired page. A second method is to drag the Point to File icon to a file within the Files panel.

2 Link to an external page by typing or copying and pasting the full Web address (a fully formed URL) in the Link field of the Properties panel.

3 A standard page link opens a new page or moves the view to a position somewhere on the page. An e-mail link opens a blank e-mail message window if the user uses an e-mail application.

4 All the work of setting up the style rules to make a list appear like a horizontal or vertical menu bar has been done for you. All the work of writing the JavaScript to make pop-up submenus work has been done for you.

5 Spry Tabbed Panels organize a variety of information into a compact, tabbed format.

6 ADDING INTERACTIVITY

In this lesson, you'll add Web 2.0 functionality to your web pages by doing the following:

- Use Dreamweaver behaviors
- Apply a behavior using Spry effects
- Work with XML data and data sources
- Insert a Spry table and a Spry Accordion widget

 This lesson will take about 60 minutes to complete. Be sure you have copied the Lessons/lesson06 folder from the *Adobe Dreamweaver CS4 Classroom in a Book* CD to your hard drive before you begin.

Our Clients

Company Anon installs
microwave transmission
equipment worldwide.

Our Corporate Clients

These companies put their trust in us to take care of their travel
needs. We can do the same for you!

Company	Tagline	Desc	Work	Startdate
Company Anon	Microwave technology for signal propogation	Company Anon is the most sophisticated tele communication company in North America, known for its high-end connectivity.	• Corporate rebranding • Web site redesign • Full identity makeover including	2005

See Santorini's Best

Santorini is perfect for
beautiful beaches and
fun-filled sunshine.

Check our recommended
hotels.

Paradise by the Sea

Welcome to Santorini

Welcome to Paradise! Santorini is Greece's most famous island
for good reason. The scenic beauty, the stunning sunsets, the
picturesque village and the friendly people all combine to create

Dreamweaver creates sophisticated interactive effects
with behaviors, data sets, and accordion panels using
the Spry Framework for Ajax.

Learning about Dreamweaver behaviors

A Dreamweaver *behavior* is JavaScript code that performs an action, such as opening a browser window, when it is triggered by an event, such as a mouse click. Applying a behavior is a three-step process:

1 Select the page element that you want to trigger the behavior.

2 Choose the behavior to apply.

3 Specify the settings or parameters of the behavior.

Typically, the triggering element involves a link, which can be attached to a range of text or to an image. In some cases, the behavior does not require loading a new page, so it will employ a dummy link that is represented as a hash sign (#). In Lesson 5, you used dummy links to trigger submenu pop-up items. The Spry Effect behavior you will use in this lesson does not require a link to function, but keep linking in mind when you work with other behaviors. Dreamweaver will add the appropriate code in most instances; however, you may have to create a dummy link as a trigger to make some Dreamweaver behaviors active. Dreamweaver includes more than 30 behaviors, all accessed in the Behaviors panel. Choose Window > Behaviors to view the Behaviors panel. Click the plus (+) sign in the Behavior panel to display the behaviors available for a particular selection in the Document window. Some of the functionality available to you using Dreamweaver behaviors includes the following:

- Opening a browser window

- Swapping an image's source and swapping it back for a rollover effect

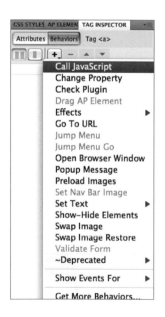

- Fading an image or page area in and out

- Growing or shrinking a graphic

- Displaying a pop-up alert message

- Changing the text or other HTML content within a given area

- Showing or hiding sections of the page

- Calling a custom-defined JavaScript function

Not all behaviors are available all the time. Certain behaviors become available only with the presence of page elements, such as images or links. For example, you'll need an image placed on a page before the Swap Image behavior is enabled in the Behaviors list.

All behaviors display a unique dialog box that defines the relevant settings. For example, the Open Browser Window dialog box allows you to set the web address of a file that you want to display in a new window, the width and height of that window, and other window attributes. The parameters can be modified at any time.

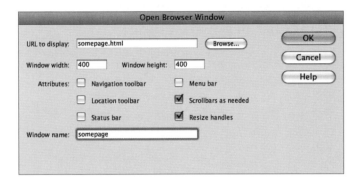

After you've defined the parameters of the behavior, it is listed in the Behaviors panel with the default triggering action displayed to the left and the name of the behavior displayed to the right. The action can be altered by choosing a different action from the Behaviors list. For example, the Open Browser Window behavior, by default, applies an onClick action; if you'd prefer a rollover trigger, you can change the action to onMouseOver.

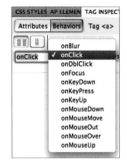

Behaviors are extremely flexible, and multiple behaviors can be applied to the same trigger. For example, you could swap one image for another and then change the text of the accompanying image caption, and do it all with one click. Although the fast response suggests that the events are simultaneous, behaviors are actually triggered in sequence. When multiple behaviors with the same triggering event are applied, you'll have the option to change the order in which the behaviors are processed by moving them up or down in the Behaviors panel.

Previewing a completed file

In this first part of this lesson, you'll work with a page about the travel agency clients. To preview the file you will work on, let's view the completed page in the browser.

1 Open Adobe Dreamweaver CS4.

2 If necessary, press F8 to open the Files panel, and choose DW CIB from the site list.

3 In the Files panel, expand the lesson06 folder.

4 Select the ourclients-finished.html file and press F12 (Windows) or Option+F12 (Mac) to preview it in your primary browser.

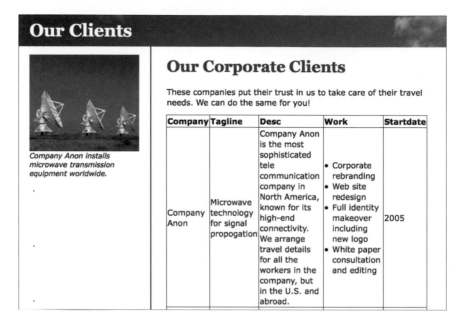

The page includes Ajax-powered effects created with Dreamweaver Spry technology.

5 If Microsoft Internet Explorer is your primary browser, a message may appear above the browser window indicating that JavaScript is prevented from running. If so, click that message, and choose Allow Blocked Content.

Move your mouse pointer over the heading, *Our Corporate Clients*. Notice that a red color highlights the headline for a brief period and then disappears. This is the result of a Spry effect called Highlight.

6 Click the column header Startdate to sort the data by year in ascending order. Click the header again to sort the data by year in descending order. Click the column header Company to sort the data in alphabetical order. The ability to sort the table according to the column headings is achieved using a Spry data set.

7 When you're done, close the browser window and return to Dreamweaver.

Using a Spry effects behavior

Spry effects can generate visual effects on a page such as highlighting elements, fading a photo in or out, or shaking an entire div like an earthquake. These effects are meant to attract attention or to highlight an element. They are dramatic effects and should be used carefully so that various parts of your page are not constantly blinking, shrinking, shaking, or flashing.

1   In the Files panel, double-click the file ourclients-start.html to open it in Dreamweaver.

2   Choose File > Save As and save the file as ourclients.html. Should you need the start page again, it will be preserved unaltered on your hard drive.

3   Spry effects can be assigned to anything currently selected in the Document window. They can also be assigned to any element with an ID. Instead of using the current selection method, let's assign an ID to an element and add a Spry effect to that element. You will add the ID using Code and Design view.

4   Position the mouse pointer anywhere in the <h1> heading, *Our Corporate Clients.*

5   Click the Split button to reveal Code and Design view.

6   In the code immediately after the h1 heading but before the closing bracket (>), insert a space and type **id="occ"**. This ID name is an abbreviation for *our corporate clients.*

7   Click the Design button to return to Design view.

8   If necessary, choose Window > Behaviors to display the Behaviors panel. Click the Plus (+) button to add a behavior. Choose Effects > Highlight.

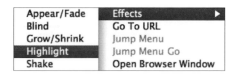

9 In the Highlight dialog box, set the Target Element to h1 "occ". Leave the default Effect duration at 1000 milliseconds. Make sure the Start Color value is #fff, the End Color value is #f00 (or #ff0000 as shown in the image), and the Color After Effect value is #fff. Click OK. The effect will be a brief red highlight behind the <h1 id="occ">element.

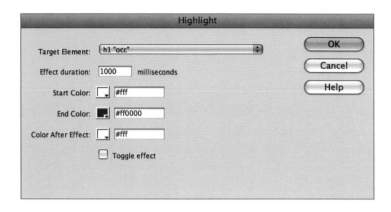

10 In the Behaviors panel, click the onClick field to activate it. Then, from the pop-up menu, choose onMouseOver.

When you want to change the parameters for the Highlight effect, double-click its name, Highlight, in the Behaviors panel to open the Highlight dialog box.

● **Note:** The effect can be deleted by selecting Highlight in the Behavior panel and clicking the Minus (-) button.

11 Use Live view or your browser to view the file. You will not see the effect unless you move your mouse pointer over the heading. Click Live View again or close your browser to return to Dreamweaver's Edit mode.

12 Save your work.

Other Spry effects can be added to a <div> or any block level element, and even made to work when the page loads. Spry effects offer a variety of attention-getting visual elements that can punch up a page and make it more appealing.

Learning about XML data

Before you can display any data sets with Spry, you'll need to establish a proper XML data source. XML (Extensible Markup Language) is a standardized specification for storing data in a text file format. Each XML file can contain multiple data records. For example, in this exercise you'll work with an XML file that holds data for a number of clients. This file is clients.xml. It contains several client records.

Each client record, without its data, looks like this:

```
<client>
    <company></company>
    <desc></desc>
    <work></work>
    <startdate></startdate>
</client>
```

XML is a markup language, as is HTML. The same tag-based method for marking up text is used in both. XML is extensible in that you can create your own tag names based on the data you are marking up.

As you'll see in the next exercise, the way the XML elements are named and arranged is referred to as the *schema*. The actual data is placed between the opening and closing tag pairs, like this:

```
<company>Company Anon</company>
```

Data that has the potential for using special characters, such as the angle brackets used to surround tags, relies on a special delimiter for character data that is used like this:

```
<desc>![CDATA[Company Anon is a <strong>bold</strong>
company.]]</desc>
```

The CDATA delimiter allows XML data to contain HTML tags. For example, the XML file used in this exercise includes a fully formatted HTML unordered list.

Importing XML data with Spry

Dreamweaver's direct route for working with the XML schema is the Spry data object, which you will work with in the following steps.

1   If necessary, in the Files panel, expand the lesson06 folder and double-click the ourclients.html file to open it. Place your mouse pointer under the paragraph in the mainContent <div> to set the insertion point for the Spry data set.

2   In the Insert panel, switch to the Spry category by choosing Spry from the Insert panel list or by clicking the Spry tab.

3   In the Spry category, click Spry Data Set 🖻. Another method is to choose Insert > Spry > Spry Data Set.

    Three steps are required to complete setting up the data set.

4   When the Spry Data Set dialog box opens, the first screen is the the Specify Data Source dialog box opens. Set the Select Data Type pop-up menu to XML. Leave the Data Set Name field as the default ds1, and click Browse.

5 In the Select XML Source dialog box, navigate to the lesson06 folder and choose clients.xml. Click Choose to close the Select XML Source dialog box. In the Row element area, choose client.

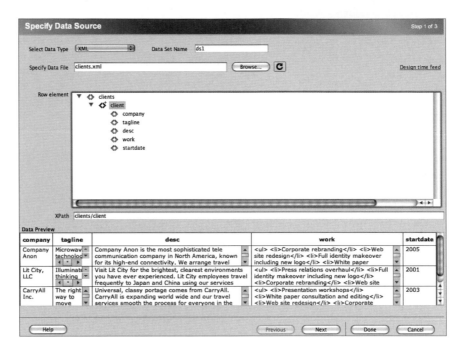

6 Click the Next button at the bottom of the dialog box to move to the second step. In the Set Data Options screen, select a data type for each column.

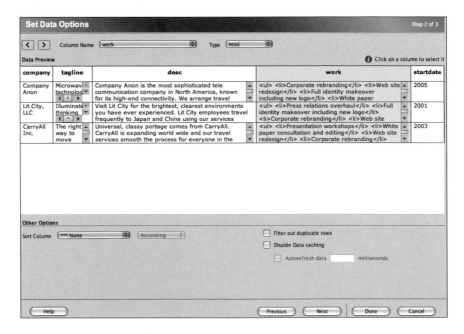

You can click in a column to see the type assigned to it. When a column is selected, data type is shown near the top in the Type menu. The default type can be changed using the pop-up menu. Types include string (basically, characters or letters), number, date, and html. The first three columns' data types can remain string. The column titled "work" must be set to html, because it contains html tags. The data type for the final column should be left as string. See the following sidebar, "Spry Data Types," for an explanation as to why it this column doesn't use a date data type.

7 Click the Next button to move to the final step. In the Choose Insert Options screen that opens, select "Insert table" and click the Set Up button.

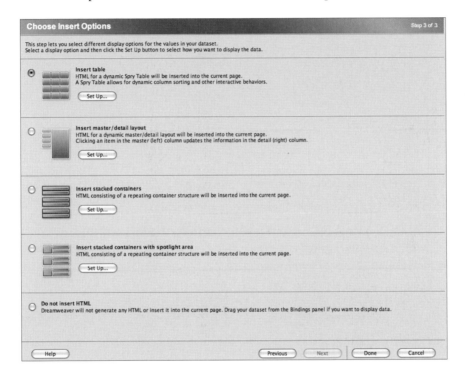

The Spry Data Set – Insert Table dialog box appears. In this dialog box, you see tools to add or remove columns, to move columns up and down, to enable column sorting, to apply classes to columns and rows, and to update detail regions when a row is clicked.

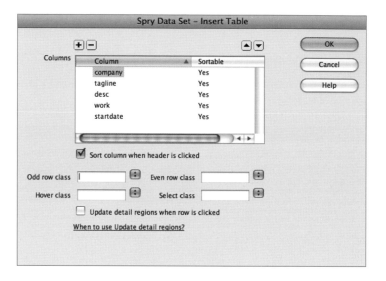

8 Click OK to accept the default settings.

You return to the Choose Insert Options dialog box.

The small table in this exercise is adequate using the default setting, but you can see the powerful sorting and display options that are provided in Spry data sets for a larger or more complex table.

9 Click Done.

Spry Data Types

The proper data type is necessary for sorting operations. The available data types are:

- string—Alphanumeric data

- number—Numeric data

- date—A full date, such as 6/13/2008 or June 13, 2008

- html—Marked-up text, such as the lists in this example

10 Choose File > Save.

Dreamweaver needs to include a couple of JavaScript files to enable Spry data functionality. The files were already present in the SpryAssets folder so that you could preview the ourclients-finished.html page. In normal circumstances, Dreamweaver would notify you about adding these files.

In Design view, you see the table with the data set placeholders. The actual data stored in the XML file will be displayed only when the page is rendered in Live view or a browser.

Besides the table and the placeholders, Dreamweaver has inserted a number of key code lines. In addition to the previously noted JavaScript files, a JavaScript function is included in the <head> tag.

11 Click the Code button to view the code. Scroll to the top of the document. At about line 25, you'll see links to JavaScripts and the function added to control the Spry data set.

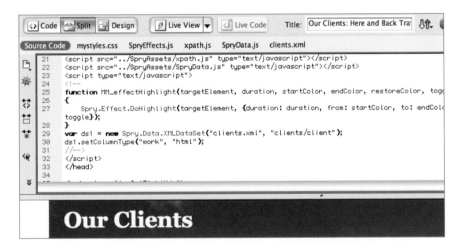

Spry data sets provide you with powerful options for importing XML or HTML source materials and displaying them dynamically on a web page using tables or containers (typically divs). Stacked containers, one of the choices in the Choose Insert Options dialog box, can include detail layouts and spotlight sections, giving you a variety of options to work with in Spry data sets.

Creating Spry Accordions

A Spry Accordion is similar to a Spry Tabbed Panel because it organizes lots of content into a compact, multi-paneled display. The tabs are stacked on top of each other, rather than side by side; so, when you click a tab, the panel slides open with a smooth action. If the content inside the panel is taller or wider than the panel itself, scroll bars appear automatically.

Preview what you will do in this exercise.

1 In the Files panel, select santorini-finished.html and press F12 (Windows) or Option+F12 (Mac) to preview it in your primary browser. The page mainContent information is in a Spry Accordion.

2 Navigate from one panel to another by clicking the headings.

3 Close your browser and return to Dreamweaver. Choose File > Close to close santorini-finished.html.

Adding a Spry Accordion

In this exercise, you'll incorporate a Spry Accordion into your layout.

1   In the Files panel, double-click santorini-start.html to open it in Dreamweaver.

2   Choose File > Save As. In the filename field, type **santorini.html**. Click Save.

The previous layout for the santorini page is preserved unaltered in the santorini-start.html file.

3   Position the mouse pointer at the end of the line *Paradise by the Sea* to establish an insertion point for the Accordion panel.

4   In the Spry category of the Insert panel, click the Spry Accordion icon .

Dreamweaver inserts the default Spry Accordion element onto the page.

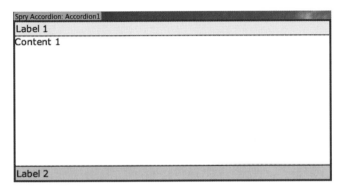

The initial element is a two-panel accordion, with the top panel exposed. A blue tab with the label *Spry Accordion: Accordion 1* and border mark the new object. Once inserted, accordion labels and content can be modified directly in Design view.

5   Choose File > Save All. If necessary, click OK to accept the files that Dreamweaver adds to the SpryAssets folder.

6   Select the placeholder phrase *Label 1* and type **Welcome to Santorini.**

7   Select the photo of the couple on the roof and all the text under it that describes the villages and the beaches. Stop before the next heading, *What Our Customers Say.*

8 To ensure that you are not leaving any stray tags behind, click the Code button.

Make sure the entire code block from the opening <p> tag before the image to the closing </ul> tag after the second list is selected. This is approximately lines 39–60.

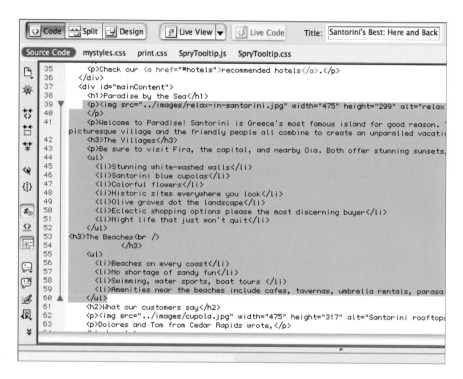

9 Click the Design button to return to Design View.

10 Choose Edit > Cut, or press Control+X (Windows) or Command+X (Mac) to copy the photo and text to the Clipboard.

11 Return to the Accordion panel. Select the text *Content 1*. Choose Edit > Paste, or press Control+V (Windows) or Command+V (Mac) to paste content into the panel.

You'll see only part of the content you added in Design view, because scrolling isn't active in Design view.

● **Note:** To hide the content so that you can work on the other panels, right-click (Windows) or Control-click (Mac) and choose Element View > Hidden, or choose Element View > Reset All Element Views.

12 To see or edit all of the content, double-click the panel, or right-click (Windows) or Control-click (Mac), and choose Element View > Full.

13 Position your mouse pointer over the gray Label 2 bar to see the eye icon. Click the eye to open panel 2.

Label 2

14 Select the Label 2 text, and type **What our customers say**.

15 Repeat steps 7 through 11 to cut the next heading, the <h2> heading, *What our customers say*, and the information under that heading. Stop before the next heading, *Recommended Hotels.* Paste it into the Content 2 panel.

One section of the page remains to be added to the Spry Accordion. You'll add a third panel for it in the next exercise.

Adding additional panels

To add or remove panels to or from the Spry Accordion , use the Properties panel.

1 Be sure the Spry Accordion *Accordion 1* is selected in the Document window.

2 In the Properties panel, click the Plus (+) button to add a panel.

Note: Panels can be removed by clicking the Minus (-) button and reordered by clicking the Up and Down arrows.

3 In the Document window, select Label 3 and type **Recommended hotels**.

4 Repeat steps 7 through 11 from the previous exercise to cut and paste the <h1> heading *Recommended hotels*, along with the photo and table, into the Content 3 panel.

5 Choose File > Save. Use Live view or press F12 (Windows) or Option+F12 (Mac) to preview the page in your primary browser.

The top panel shows by default.

6 Click the other Accordion tabs and scroll to see more contents.

7 Click the sidebar link to the recommended hotels with the Recommended Hotels panel closed. Then click the Recommended Hotels tab to open the panel. In the sidebar, click the link to the recommended hotels again. The link in the sidebar works only when the third panel is active and open.

8 Click Live View again or close the browser window to return to Edit mode.

9 Delete the sentence in the sidebar that says *Check our recommended hotels.*

The link works only when the Recommended Hotels panel is open, which can create confusion. And with the more compact access to all the page contents in the Accordion, a link to material at the bottom of a long page is not necessary.

10 Choose File > Save.

You created a Spry Accordion and added content and additional panels to it. Although the content added in this exercise was already on the page, you could to enter content and edit directly in the Content panels. You could also copy material from other sources, such as Word documents. Any type of content can be entered in the panels, in addition to the text, images, and table used in this exercise.

In the next exercise, you'll customize the CSS for the Spry Accordion.

Customizing a Spry Accordion

Like other Spry widgets, Spry Accordions have a CSS file attached. In this exercise, you will adjust the height of the content panels and change the color scheme in the label bars.

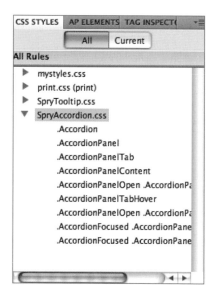

● **Note:** Some selector names are too long to display in the All Rules pane. Dreamweaver shows you the entire selector name when you place your mouse pointer over the selector.

1 In the CSS Styles panel, locate the style sheet SpryAccordion.css and expand it. You now have four external style sheets linked to this page.

2 Select .AccordionPanelTab.

3 Click the Edit Rule icon (which looks like a pencil).

4 In the "CSS Rule Definition for .AccordionPanelTab in SpryAccordion.css" dialog box, select the Type category and click the color box to open the color picker. In the color picker, change the color to white (#FFF).

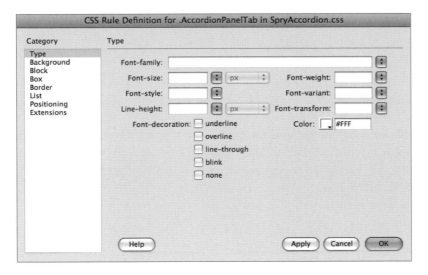

5 Select the Background category. In the Background-color field, change #CCC to #345FA3.

This is the color used in the <h1> heading just above the accordion. In the next several steps, you will change all the blue in the Spry Accordion to the color #345FA3.

6 Click OK.

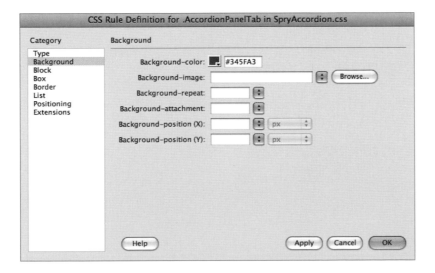

7 In the CSS styles All Rules pane, select .AccordionPanelContent. If necessary, enlarge the Properties pane just below the All Rules pane. Click in the height data field to make it editable, and change 200 to 400. Leave the menu that opens to the right set for px. Press Enter (or Return).

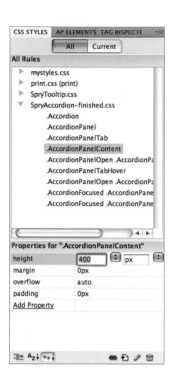

All of the content panels are set to the same height. The 400px choice allows more of the content to display before the user must scroll, but it isn't such a large height that the user may not notice additional panels under the first one. The height you choose for .AccordionPanelContent depends on the amount of content you will display in any particular case.

8 In the All Rules pane, select ".AccordionPanel Open .AccordionPanelTab." In the Properties pane, click the background-color field to make it editable and type **#345FA3**. Press Enter (or Return).

9 Click the Add Property link. Type **color** for the property name and type **#FFF** for the color value. Press Enter (or Return).

10 In the All Rules pane, select .AccordionPanelTabHover. In the Properties pane, click the color box and use the color picker to select yellow (#FF0) for the tab hover color.

You will now change several more colors by editing a color value in the Properties pane.

11 In the All Rules pane, select ".AccordionPanelOpen .AccordionPanelTabHover." In the Properties pane, repeat the process you used in step 10 to change the value for the open panel tab hover color to yellow (#FF0).

12 In the All Rules pane, select ".AccordionFocused .AccordionPanelTab." (*Focus* refers to the state of the tab when it's the active panel.) In the Properties pane, repeat the process described in step 8 to change the default blue background color to #345FA3.

13 Finally, in the All Rules pane, select ".AccordionFocused .AccordionPanelOpen .AccordionPanelTab." In the Properties pane, change the default blue background color to #345FA3.

You've successfully created a color scheme for the Accordion panel that matches the web page colors. You changed the height of the content panes to allow more content to display before the user must scroll to read it all.

Review questions

1 True or false: XML is a method for storing data in a plain-text file for use in web applications

2 What is a benefit of using Spry effects?

3 What is a benefit of using Spry data sets to add tables to a web page?

4 What does a Spry Accordion do?

Review answers

1 True. XML is a mark-up language similar to HTML, in which the data is tagged and structured in a plain-text, non-proprietary file format.

2 Spry effects create a focal point on a page by visually highlighting, fading in and out, or shaking to bring attention to a page element.

3 Spry data sets add XML or HTML information to a page in a table format, complete with sortable columns and other advanced properties. This allows users to interact with the data live on the page.

4 A Spry Accordion includes two or more collapsible panels that hide and reveal content in a contained area of the page.

7 CREATING A PAGE LAYOUT

In this lesson, you'll build CSS-based page layouts from start to finish and accomplish the following:

- Define CSS rules for layout areas

- Apply CSS rules to inserted <div> tags

- Add text and image placeholders to the page

- Export internal CSS rules to an external style sheet

- Work with Code view and Code Navigator

- Use rulers and guides to fine-tune a layout

- Check your layout for browser compatibility and validity

This lesson will take about 60 minutes to complete. Be sure you have copied Lessons > lesson07 from the *Adobe Dreamweaver CS4 Classroom in a Book* CD to your hard drive before beginning. As you work on this lesson, you'll overwrite the start files. Unlike other lessons, the work you do here will not become a page for the travel site. If you need to restore the start files, recopy them from the CD to your hard drive.

Logo (760 x 71)

Navigation (760 x 28)

Banner (760 x 200)

Main Heading

Subheading

{width: 365px
float: left}
Lorem ipsum dolor sit amet, consetetur sadipscing elitr, sed
diam nonumy eirmod tempor invidunt ut labore et dolore
magna aliquyam erat, sed diam voluptua. At vero eos et
accusam et justo duo dolores et ea rebum. Stet clita kasd
gubergren, no sea takimata sanctus est Lorem ipsum dolor
sit amet.

Subheading

{width: 365px;
float: right;}
Lorem ipsum dolor sit amet, consetetur sadipscing elitr, sed
diam nonumy eirmod tempor invidunt ut labore et dolore
magna aliquyam erat, sed diam voluptua. At vero eos et
accusam et justo duo dolores et ea rebum. Stet clita kasd
gubergren, no sea takimata sanctus est Lorem ipsum dolor
sit amet.

Content for id "footer" Goes Here

Dreamweaver creates standards-based CSS
to help web designers meet the challenges
of building layouts with styles.

Previewing a completed file

To understand the layout you will work on in the first part of this lesson, preview the completed page in the browser.

1   Open Adobe Dreamweaver CS4.

2   If necessary, press F8 to open the Files panel, and choose DW CIB from the site list.

3   In the Files panel, expand the lesson07 folder.

4   Double-click the layout_final.html file to open it.

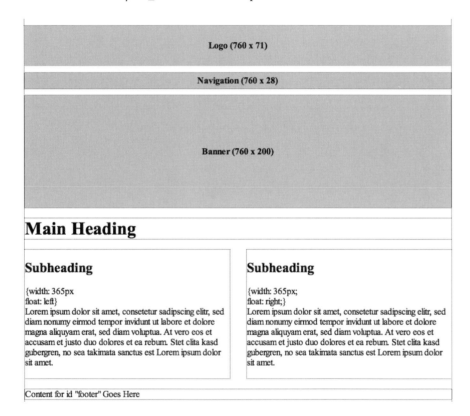

This page represents the layout you will create in this lesson. In some ways it is similar to the layout for the travel pages, but it's sufficiently different to give you experience crafting a fresh page layout in a fixed-width design. The two columns are created by floating one `<div>` element to the left and one to the right.

By comparison, the layout for the travel pages uses float:left to create the sidebar, and a wide margin-left value on the Main Content to provide space for a single floated <div>.

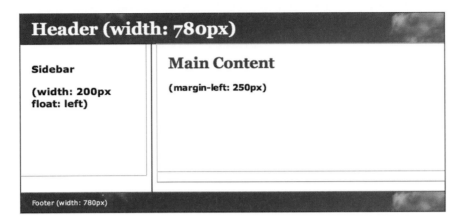

Both layouts use clear:both in the footer <div> to move the footer to the bottom of the container. This is due to the application of float to one or both of the <div> elements preceding the footer.

5   Choose File > Close.

Creating layout styled <div> elements

Best practices for today's web designer advocate CSS-based layouts. A CSS-based layout—compared with a table-based layout—reduces file size, is easier to manage, and meets industry standards. CSS-based layouts have two basic components: a set of <div> elements that create a page structure that is useful on its own, and a series of CSS rules that define the dimensions and format of key page elements so that the page assumes a functional and attractive appearance.

Creating the page and defining the body tag

In this exercise, you'll build a CSS-based layout from a blank HTML document. After the file is created, you'll declare your first CSS rule for the <body> tag.

1   Choose File > New. When the New Document dialog box opens, choose Blank Page. From the Page Type column, choose HTML, and from the Layout column, choose <none>. (Notice that no Layout CSS options are available for a blank page.) Click Create.

Note: If the Dreamweaver Welcome screen is displayed, a quicker way to create a blank HTML page is to click the first entry, HTML, in the Create New column.

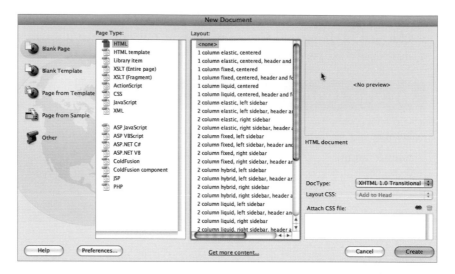

2   Choose File > Save. In the Save As dialog box, navigate to the lesson07 folder, and in the File Name field, type **layout_start.html**. Click OK (Windows) or Save (Mac).

3   Choose Window > CSS Styles. When the CSS Styles panel opens, switch to All mode, if necessary, by clicking All.

4   At the bottom of the CSS Styles panel, click New CSS Rule.

It's a good idea to begin with the basics for your layout by first defining a CSS rule for the <body> tag.

● **Note:** Many web professionals initially define their CSS layout rules in the <head> of the layout document. This practice simplifies development and eliminates the need to work with multiple files. After the design is complete, the rules are exported to an external style sheet, as described later in this lesson.

5   When the New CSS Rule dialog box appears, from the Selector Type pop–up menu, choose "Tag (redefines an HTML element)." In the Selector Name field, choose "body" from the pop-up menu or type **body**. From the Rule Definition pop-up menu, choose "(This document only)" and click OK.

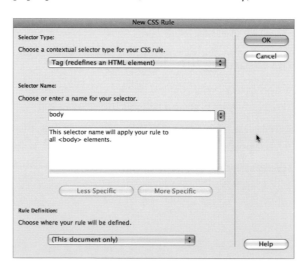

6 In the "CSS Rule definition for body" dialog box, choose the Background category. Click the color box to open the color picker, and with the eyedropper tool click the white swatch.

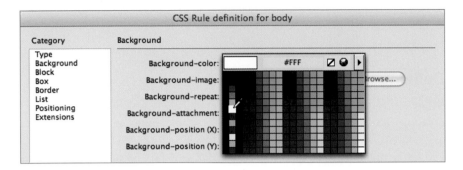

7 In the Category column, click Block. From the "Text align" list, choose center.

The layout under construction will be centered in the browser window, although the text will be aligned left. To render properly in older browsers, such as Microsoft Internet Explorer 5.x, you first need to set the "Text-align" property to center in the overarching <body> tag. A later CSS rule re-aligns the text to the left for items within a containing tag.

8 Choose the Box category. In the Padding area, type **0** in the Top field. In the Margin area, type **0** in the Top field. Click OK.

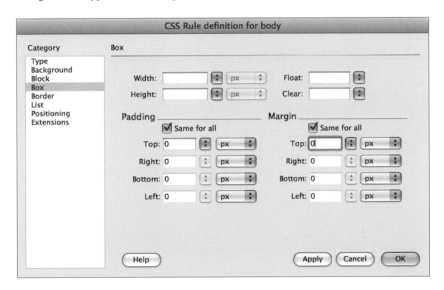

9 Choose File > Save.

The background color is set to white, and both the Padding and Margin properties are at 0. Since all HTML elements are styled by the browser with varying amounts of Padding and Margin, initially setting them all to 0 gives you control over these values, as required by your design. You're ready to define the layout containers for the page.

Defining the outer wrapper

While <div> tags can be used throughout a web layout, a standard technique for creating CSS-based designs is to use a <div> tag to contain, or *wrap*, all other tags and content. These *wrappers* help establish global settings, such as overall width and layout alignments. In this exercise, you'll define the CSS rule for such a wrapper and insert the associated <div> tag.

1 If necessary, open the layout_start.html file by double-clicking its entry in the Files panel.

2 In the CSS Styles panel, click New CSS Rule.

3 When the New CSS Rule dialog box opens, from the Selector Type pop-up menu, choose "ID (applies to only one HTML element)." In the Selector Name field, type **#wrapper** (or the name of your choice.) In the Rule Definition pop-up menu, verify that "(This document only)" is chosen. Click OK.

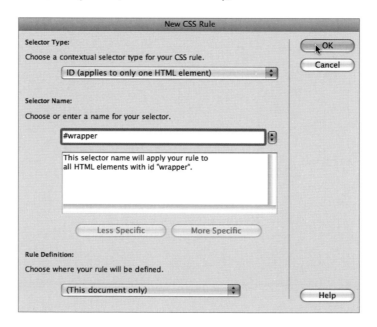

● **Note:** Dreamweaver remembers settings from the last time you created a new CSS rule. In many cases, you won't need to change particular parameters, such as the Rule Definition.

You'll recall from Lesson 2 that the leading hash mark indicates an ID selector that can be applied only once per page.

4 In the "CSS Rule Definition for #wrapper" dialog box, choose the Block category. In the Text-align pop-up menu, choose left.

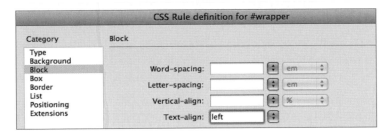

In the previous exercise, the rule for the <body> tag set the Text align property to center to maintain compatibility with older browsers. Because an ID selector such as #wrapper has more importance (*specificity*) in the style rules than the <body> tag selector, all elements eventually placed in the #wrapper <div> tag will be left-aligned and not centered.

● **Note:** To learn more about how the importance of CSS selectors is determined, see "Understanding Specificity" at www.adobe.com/devnet/dreamweaver/articles/css_specificity.html.

5 Choose the Box category. In the Width field, type **760**, and press Tab. In the Margin area, deselect the "Same for all" check box. In the Top field, type **0**, and press Tab. From the Right pop-up menu, choose auto. In the Bottom field, type **0**, and press Tab. From the Left pop-up menu, choose auto. Click OK.

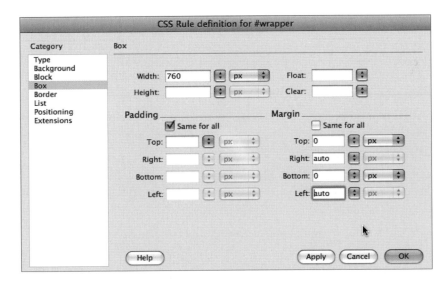

This layout design calls for a set width of 760 pixels, which works well for a screen size of 800 x 600 pixels. Why not use a width of 800 pixels? The 40 extra pixels are used to display the sides of the browser including any necessary scroll bars. This area of the browser, along with sections above and below the main viewing window, is referred to as *chrome*.

The left and right margins are set to auto to center the #wrapper <div> and, therefore, the contained page content. In this exercise, if the browser window is larger than the 760-pixel set width, the remaining width is divided and equally applied to the left and right margins, automatically.

Now you're ready to insert the <div> tag with the #wrapper style. As you'll recall from working with the about.html page .profile <div>, Dreamweaver offers a direct approach for adding a <div> and assigning it an ID or CSS class.

6 In the Layout category of the Insert panel, click Insert Div Tag. When the Insert Div Tag dialog box opens, select "At insertion point," if necessary. From the ID pop-up menu, choose wrapper, and click OK.

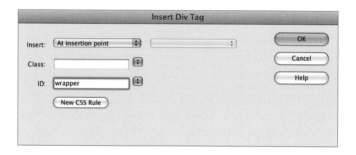

● **Note:** If you don't see a dashed outline around the newly inserted <div> tag, on the Document toolbar click the Visual Aids menu button, and choose CSS Layout Outlines.

Dreamweaver adds the new <div> to the page with placeholder content that reads *Content for id "wrapper" Goes Here*.

7 Press F4 to close all panels and display the Document window fully. Notice that the outlined <div> tag, #wrapper, is centered in the Document window. Press F4 again to redisplay the panels, and choose File > Save.

The #wrapper <div> tag typically serves as a container for other <div> tags rather than text or images. The purpose of the wrapper <div> is to constrain the width of the layout.

Now that the outer wrapper is in place, you'll add the major layout divisions.

Setting up the primary divisions

The current design will be divided into three major areas: header, content section, and footer. Each of these areas requires a separate CSS rule and <div> tag.

1 If necessary, open the layout_start.html by double-clicking its filename in the Files panel.

To start, define the first of our CSS rules, #header.

2 In the CSS Styles panel, click New CSS Rule. When the New CSS Rule dialog box appears, in the Selector Name field, type **#header**. Verify that in the Selector Type pop-up menu, "ID (applies to only one HTML element)" is chosen, and in the Rule Definition pop-up menu, "(This document only)" is chosen. Click OK.

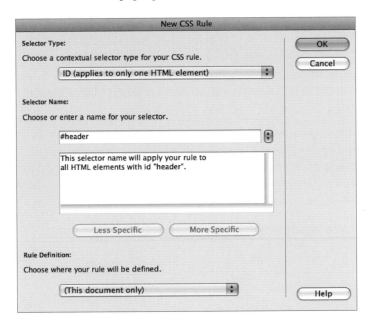

3 In the "CSS Rule definition for #header" dialog box, choose the Box category. In the Margin area, deselect the "Same for all" check box. In the Top field, type **12**, and press Tab. In the Bottom field, type **12**, and press Tab. Click OK.

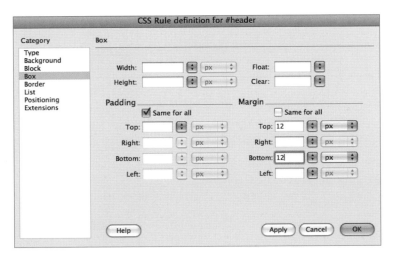

When applied, the #header CSS rule will provide a little bit of space above and below the <div> tag. It's not necessary to declare a width because, by default, an HTML block element such as a <div> tag expands to fill its container—which will be, in this case, the #wrapper <div> tag.

Continue to define the other two desired CSS rules.

4 In the CSS Styles panel, click New CSS Rule. When the New CSS Rule dialog box appears, in the Selector Name field, type **#content**. Verify that in the Selector Type pop-up menu, "ID (applies to only one HTML element)" is chosen, and that the Rule Definition pop-up menu is set to "(This document only)." Click OK.

5 In the "CSS Rule definition for #content" dialog box, choose the Box category. In the Padding area, deselect the "Same for all" check box, and type **0** in the Top field. In the Margin area, deselect the "Same for all" check box and type **0** in the Top field. Click OK. These settings will cause the content to appear immediately under the header with no white space.

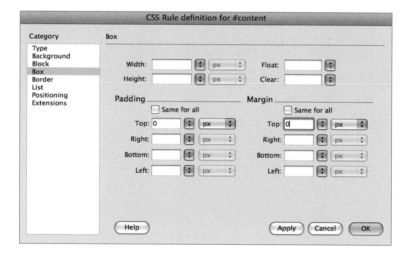

The final CSS rule to declare, #footer, is sufficiently similar to the #header rule that you can take a shortcut to create it.

6 In the CSS Styles panel, right-click (Windows) or Control-click (Mac) the #header style, and from the context menu, choose Duplicate.

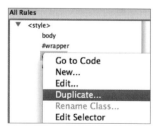

7 When the Duplicate CSS Rule dialog box appears, in the Selector Name field, type **#footer**, and click OK.

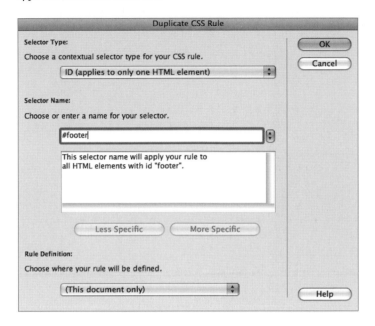

When you duplicate an existing style rule, the new rule is inserted without the "CSS Rule definition" dialog box appearing. If you need to make any adjustments, you can use the Properties pane of the CSS Styles panel.

8 In the All Rules pane of the CSS Styles panel, select #footer, and in the Properties pane, click Add Property. In the first column, type **clear**, and press Tab. From the second column pop-up menu, choose both.

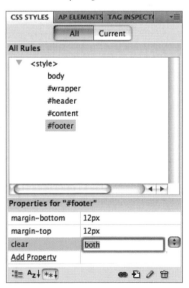

The `clear:both` CSS property ensures that no floated elements will intrude on the #footer. As you'll see later in this lesson, the #content area <div> will contain two floated <div> tags.

Now that the CSS rules for the major layout areas are defined, you can add them to the page, starting with the #header.

9 Select the placeholder text, *Content for id "wrapper" Goes Here*, and press Delete to remove it.

10 In the Insert panel, click Insert Div Tag. In the Insert Div Tag dialog box, from the Insert pop-up menu, choose "After start of tag," and then, from the adjacent pop-up menu, choose "<div id="wrapper">." From the ID pop-up menu, choose header, and click OK.

By inserting the #header <div> tag after the start of the #wrapper <div> tag, you are nesting one <div> tag inside another and your code will look like this:

```
<div id="wrapper>
    <div id="header"> Content for id "header" Goes Here
    </div>
</div>
```

Now, add two more layout <div> tags, each contained within the #wrapper <div> tag.

11 In the Insert panel, click Insert Div Tag. In the Insert Div Tag dialog box, from the Insert pop-up menu, choose "After tag," and from the adjacent pop-up menu, choose "<div id="header">." From the ID pop-up menu, choose content, and click OK.

Notice that each time you choose an item from the ID pop-up menu, only the unassigned ID selectors are available. By limiting your choices, Dreamweaver prevents you from reusing an ID.

12 In the Insert panel, click Insert Div Tag. In the Insert Div Tag dialog box, from the Insert pop-up menu, choose "After tag," and from the adjacent pop-up menu, choose "`<div id="content">`." From the ID pop-up menu, choose footer, and click OK.

The placeholder text makes it easy to see where each major layout division is situated.

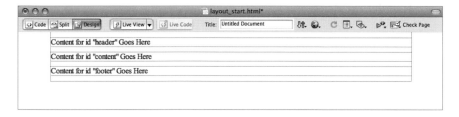

13 In the Title field of the Document toolbar, type **Layout**, and press Enter (Windows) or Return (Mac).

14 Choose File > Save.

In the next exercise, you'll expand on the basic layout by including a number of more targeted content areas.

Adding content areas

While it's entirely possible to use the basic layout that you've constructed so far in this lesson, the resulting page might be a little bland. More sophisticated designs include additional content areas placed adjacent to a layout `<div>` tag or nested within one. In this exercise, you'll work with both scenarios.

1 If necessary, open the layout_start.html file by double-clicking its entry in the Files panel.

First, define the CSS rule for a `<div>` tag to hold the logo.

2 In the CSS Styles panel, click New CSS Rule. When the New CSS Rule dialog box appears, in the Selector Name field, type **#logo**. Verify that the Selector Type pop-up menu is set to "ID (applies to only one HTML element)" and that the Rule Definition pop-up menu is set to "(This document only)." Click OK.

In this design, the planned logo is a background image that measures 760 pixels in width and 71 pixels in height. A height must be specified so that the full graphic will be seen. A little bit of padding is also needed to separate the logo from other elements.

3 When the "CSS Rule definition for #logo" dialog box appears, choose the Box category. In the Height field, type **71**. In the Padding area, deselect the "Same for all" check box, and in the Bottom field, type **12**. Click OK.

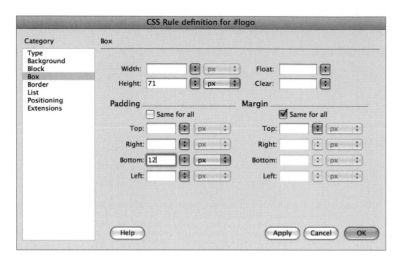

Now you can add the #logo <div> tag in its proper place within the #header <div> tag.

4 In the Insert panel, click Insert Div Tag. In the Insert Div Tag dialog box, from the Insert pop-up menu, choose "After start of tag," and from the adjacent pop-up menu, choose "<div id="header">." From the ID pop-up menu, choose logo, and click OK.

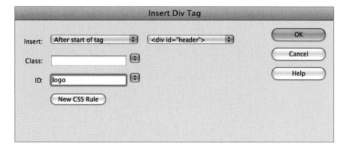

Because you've started to put content in the header <div> tag, the placeholder text is no longer needed and can be removed.

5 Select the placeholder text, *Content for id "header" Goes Here*, and press Delete.

Now add one more styled element to the #header <div> tag—an area to hold the main navigation. Because the CSS rule is quite similar to that of #logo, you can take the Duplicate shortcut.

6 In the CSS Styles panel, right-click (Windows) or Control-click (Mac) the #logo style, and from the context menu, choose Duplicate. When the Duplicate CSS Rule dialog box appears, in the Selector Name field, type **#nav**, and click OK.

Next, you'll specify a different height for the #nav <div> tag and eliminate the unneeded padding-bottom property.

7 In the All Rules pane of the CSS Styles panel, choose #nav. In the CSS Styles Properties pane, first change the height value from 71 to 28, and then select the padding-bottom property and click the trash can icon at the lower right of the CSS Styles panel.

The #nav <div> tag will be nested within the #header <div> tag, but also—and more important—directly *after* the #logo <div> tag.

8 In the Insert panel, click Insert Div Tag. In the Insert Div Tag dialog box, from the Insert pop-up menu, choose "After tag," and from the adjacent pop-up menu, choose "<div id="logo">." From the ID pop-up menu, choose nav, and click OK.

Not all content areas are nested within primary layout <div> tags. Next, you'll create a style for a banner to be placed between the header and content areas. Again, the quickest way is to duplicate an existing style and modify it.

9 In the CSS Styles panel, right-click (Windows) or Control-click (Mac) the #nav style, and from the context menu, choose Duplicate. When the Duplicate CSS Rule dialog box appears, in the Selector Name field, type **#banner**, and click OK.

10 In the All Rules pane of the CSS Styles panel, select #banner. In the CSS Styles Properties pane, change the height value from 28 to 200.

11 In the Insert panel, click Insert Div Tag. In the Insert Div Tag dialog box, from the Insert pop-up menu, choose "After tag," and from the adjacent pop-up menu, choose "`<div id="header">`." From the ID pop-up menu, choose banner, and click OK.

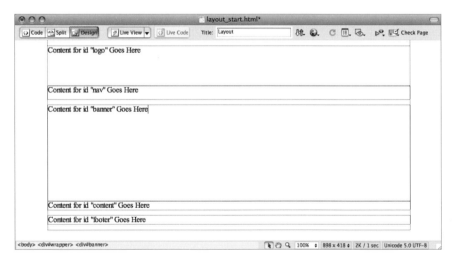

The page is really beginning to take shape now! The next evolution of the design is to separate the content area into two columns. To accomplish this goal, you'll first need to define a style for each column.

12 In the CSS Styles panel, click New CSS Rule. When the New CSS Rule dialog box appears, in the Selector Name field, type **#leftColumn**. Verify that the Selector Type pop-up menu is set to ID (applies to only one HTML element} and that the Rule Definition pop-up menu is set to "This document only." Click OK.

13 When the "CSS Rule definition for #leftColumn" dialog box opens, select the Box category. In the Width field, type **365**, and press Tab. From the Float pop-up menu, choose left. Click OK.

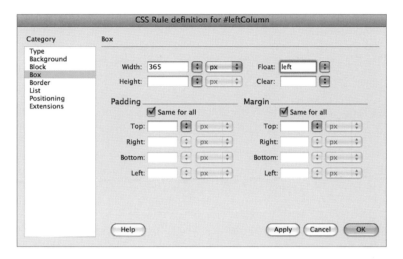

One key technique for creating columns with CSS is to use the float property. As you may remember, a floated element moves to one side of the containing element and allows other content to flow around it. This is how right-aligned or left-aligned images—and columns—are styled.

By design, these columns are quite similar, so the Duplicate method is again fastest.

14 In the CSS Styles panel, right-click (Windows) or Control-click (Mac) the #leftColumn style, and from the context menu, choose Duplicate. When the Duplicate CSS Rule dialog box is displayed, enter **#rightColumn** in the Selector Name field and click OK.

15 In the All Rules pane of the CSS Styles panel, select #rightColumn. In the Properties pane, change the float value from left to right.

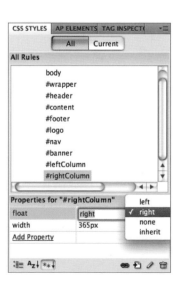

You're almost done! The final steps in this portion of the exercise are to add the styled <div> tags to the page.

16 In the Insert panel, click Insert Div Tag. In the Insert Div Tag dialog box, from the Insert pop-up menu, choose "After start of tag," and from the adjacent pop-up menu, choose "`<div id="content">`." From the ID pop-up menu, choose leftColumn, and click OK.

Like the #logo `<div>` tag, the #rightColumn is within a containing tag, #content, and follows another nested `<div>` tag, #leftColumn.

17 Click Insert Div Tag. In the Insert Div Tag dialog box, from the Insert pop-up menu, choose "After tag," and from the adjacent pop-up menu, choose "`<div id="leftColumn">`." From the ID pop-up menu, choose rightColumn, and click OK.

All that's left to do is a little clean-up.

18 Select the placeholder text, *Content for id "content" Goes Here*, and press Delete.

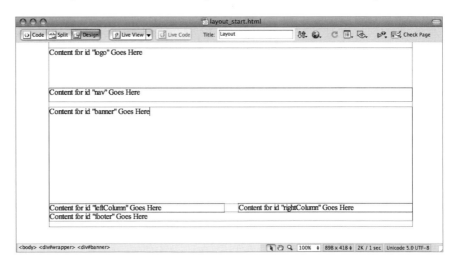

19 Choose File > Save.

Although you could hand this page to a designer as it stands, it might take her a bit of effort to figure out what you intended. A good way to create a clean layout design, ready for content, is to add more visual placeholders—a task you'll undertake in the next exercise.

Inserting placeholders

In this exercise, you'll flesh out the layout design with two kinds of placeholder content: image and text.

1 If necessary, open the layout_start.html file by double-clicking its entry in the Files panel.

2 Select the placeholder text, *Content for id "logo" Goes Here*, and press Delete. In the Common category of the Insert panel, click the Images button, and from the pop-up menu, choose Image Placeholder.

3 When the Image Placeholder dialog box opens, enter **Logo** in the Name field, **760** in the Width field, and **71** in the Height field. Leave all the other fields at their default values, and click OK.

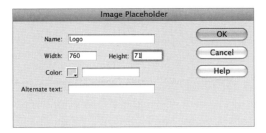

The same process is used to create placeholders for the #nav and #banner <div> tags.

4 Repeat steps 2 and 3 to replace the placeholder text in the #nav <div> tag with an image placeholder named Navigation, with a width of 760 and height of 28.

5 Repeat steps 2 and 3 once more to replace the placeholder text in the #banner <div> tag with an image placeholder named Banner, with a width of 760 and a height of 200.

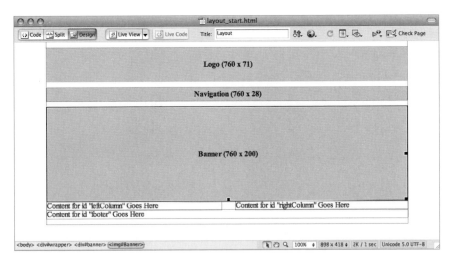

With graphic placeholders inserted, you'll add some basic placeholder text, starting with a headline that spans both columns.

6   Place your mouse pointer in the placeholder text *Content for id "leftColumn" Goes Here*, and from the tag selector, choose `<div #leftColumn>`. In the Document window, press the Left Arrow key to move the pointer position to immediately before the `<div #leftColumn>`. Type **Main Heading**. The text will appear in the Document within the `#content` `<div>`, but before the first sidebar `<div>`. Choose Window > Properties to open the Properties panel, and from the Format pop-up menu, choose Heading 1.

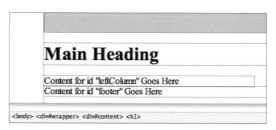

7   Select the placeholder text *Content for id "leftColumn" Goes Here* and type **Subheading**. In the Properties panel, from the Format pop-up menu, choose Heading 2. Place your mouse pointer after the just-entered text, and press Enter (Windows) or Return (Mac) to create a new line below the heading.

To spare you the chore of typing in a paragraph of placeholder text, a file has been created that you can copy and paste into the page.

8   In the Files panel, expand lesson07 and double-click placeholder_text.html to open it. Choose Edit > Select All, and then press Control+C (Windows) or Command+C (Mac); then choose File > Close. Return to layout_start.html and press Control+V (Windows) or Command+V (Mac) to paste the copied text.

Main Heading

Content for id "rightColumn" Goes Here

Subheading

Lorem ipsum dolor sit amet, consetetur sadipscing elitr, sed diam nonumy eirmod tempor invidunt ut labore et dolore magna aliquyam erat, sed diam voluptua. At vero eos et accusam et justo duo dolores et ea rebum. Stet clita kasd gubergren, no sea takimata sanctus est Lorem ipsum dolor sit amet.

You can put the exact same content into the right column with a quick and easy shortcut.

9   With your mouse pointer in the left column, choose Edit > Select All. Notice that only the text within the `#leftColumn` `<div>` tag is selected. Press

Control+C (Windows) or Command+C (Mac) to copy the text. Select the placeholder text *Content for id "rightColumn" Goes Here*, and press Control+V (Windows) or Command+V (Mac) to paste the copied content.

Main Heading

Subheading

Lorem ipsum dolor sit amet, consetetur sadipscing elitr, sed diam nonumy eirmod tempor invidunt ut labore et dolore magna aliquyam erat, sed diam voluptua. At vero eos et accusam et justo duo dolores et ea rebum. Stet clita kasd gubergren, no sea takimata sanctus est Lorem ipsum dolor sit amet.

Subheading

Lorem ipsum dolor sit amet, consetetur sadipscing elitr, sed diam nonumy eirmod tempor invidunt ut labore et dolore magna aliquyam erat, sed diam voluptua. At vero eos et accusam et justo duo dolores et ea rebum. Stet clita kasd gubergren, no sea takimata sanctus est Lorem ipsum dolor sit amet.

In Dreamweaver, the Select All command initially selects the content within a container, such as text in a table cell or content in a `<div>` tag. This allows you to quickly copy or move content from one location to another.

Use the Select All command once again to select the container, and a third time to select everything on the page.

10 Choose File > Save.

Now your layout design is both structurally sound and easy to follow.

Looking at Code view

Dreamweaver makes it as easy to work with a page in Code view as in Design view. Often a task is actually easier to accomplish in Code view or Code and Design view than in Design view alone. In Lesson 1, you used Code and Design view to see two versions of your page in a horizontal or vertical split view. In this exercise, you'll learn more about code and use the Code Navigator.

1 Open layout_final.html in Dreamweaver. It has the external style sheet needed for this exercise.

2 Click Code to view the code.

3 Choose View > Code View Options, and individually choose Word Wrap, Line Numbers, and Syntax Coloring if they are not currently chosen.

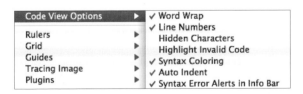

4 To select a code section, place your pointer anywhere in the tag, `<div id="leftColumn">`.

5 In the tag selector, click `<div#leftColumn>`.

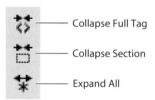

The entire `<div>` is selected and can be copied, moved, or collapsed. The markers next to the line numbers indicate that lines 20–25 are selected and can be manipulated as a section.

Code sections are often collapsed when developers are looking for a particular element or section of a page and they want to temporarily hide unneeded code sections from view. Use the collapse and expand icons on the toolbar to the left to collapse or expand sections of code.

6 Click the Collapse Section icon to collapse the selected `<div>`. Lines 20–25 will collapse into a compact marker. Click the Expand All icon to restore the lines to view.

```
20  ▶        <div id...
26
```

Code can be added or edited in Code view.

7 Find this bit of code: float: left}
.

8 Delete the `<br />` and type `</`.

9 Type `</`.

Notice that Dreamweaver's code completion function completes the tag for you by completing the `</p>` tag. The completed paragraph now includes the following:

```
<p>{width: 365px<br />
    float: left}</p>
```

10 Choose Edit > Undo to return to the <br /> tag. Watch the code, you may need to choose Edit > Undo more than once to return to the previous state.

11 Place your mouse pointer anywhere in the tag <div id="header">. In the toolbar to the left of the Document window, click the Code Navigator icon (which looks like a ship's steering wheel).

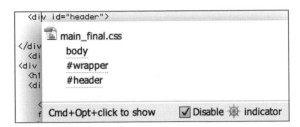

You can see information about the attached CSS for this tag in this view. Notice the light gray underline for items that have links to more information.

12 To dismiss the Code Navigator box, click anywhere outside the box.

13 Click again to open the Code Navigator. Position your mouse pointer over a linked item, and a tooltip appears with more information.

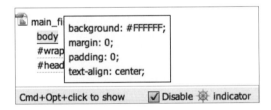

14 Click a link, and you'll jump straight into the relevant linked file—in this case, main_final.css.

15 Click the Source Code button at the top of the Document window to return to the source Code view.

Code Navigator functions

Code Navigator is useful in many situations, most of which you haven't yet experienced in these exercises. As you learn about templates, library items, and other Dreamweaver features in future exercises, keep the Code Navigator functions in mind.

If you invoke Code Navigator from a child instance of a template, Code Navigator will list the parent template .dwt file.

If you invoke Code Navigator inside a library item element on a page, Code Navigator will list the library item .lbi file.

If you invoke Code Navigator inside a server-side include (SHTML, PHP, ColdFusion, ASP & ASP.NET includes), Code Navigator will list a target link for the include file and take you to the beginning of the include file.

If you invoke Code Navigator inside a `<script>` tag, Code Navigator will list the external JavaScript file and take you to the beginning of the file.

If you invoke Code Navigator inside an iframe, Code Navigator will list the source file if it resides locally and take you to the beginning of the file.

16 Click immediately after this code block:

```
<div id="rightColumn">

    <h2>Subheading</h2>

    <p>{width: 365px;<br />

    float: right;}<br />

    Lorem ipsum dolor sit amet, consetetur sadipscing elitr,
sed diam nonumy eirmod tempor invidunt ut labore et dolore
magna aliquyam erat, sed diam voluptua. At vero eos et accusam
et justo duo dolores et ea rebum. Stet clita kasd gubergren, no
sea takimata sanctus est Lorem ipsum dolor sit amet.</p></div>
```

17 Choose Insert > Comment.

An HTML comment block appears with the pointer positioned in the center, where you will type a comment.

18 Type **end of rightColumn div**.

The completed comment will appear:

```
<!-end of rightColumn div-->
```

HTML comments do not appear in the browser, but are visible in Code view to provide helpful information and tips for yourself or any other developers who might use the file.

You have used a number of techniques to make working with code easier and more efficient. You have collapsed code, changed the HTML tags used, tried the Code Navigator, and added an HTML comment to the code.

Exporting CSS styles

The layout page that you worked on in layout_start.html is now complete unto itself. However, before this page is put into production, it's a good idea to move the CSS styles from the <head> of the document to an external CSS style sheet. An internal style sheet is limited to one page. An external style sheet can be linked to any number of pages. Dreamweaver offers a command to handle that task quickly and easily.

1 If necessary, open the layout_start.html file by double-clicking its entry in the Files panel.

2 In the CSS Styles panel, select the first defined style, body; hold down Shift; and select the last style, #rightColumn.

3 In the CSS Styles panel, from the Options menu in the upper right corner, choose Move CSS Rules.

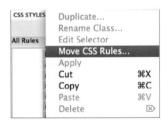

You could also right-click (Windows) or Control-click (Mac) the selected area to reach the same menu option.

4 When the Move To External Style Sheet dialog box appears, in the Move Rules To options, choose "A new style sheet," and click OK.

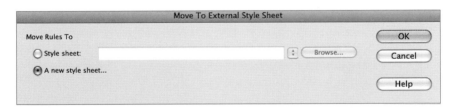

5 In the Save Style Sheet File As dialog box, navigate to the lesson07 folder, and in the File Name field, type **main.css**.

6 Click Save.

Dreamweaver moves the selected styles from the <head> area to the newly defined style sheet, and it simultaneously inserts a link to the style sheet from the current document.

The last chore is to remove the no-longer-needed <style> tag.

7 In the CSS Styles panel, click the <style> entry and press Delete, or click the trash can button.

8 Choose File > Save All.

In the next exercise, you'll use Dreamweaver's ruler and guides to make adjustments to your layouts.

Using the ruler and guides

Designs are rarely static. Changes can come from any quarter—the client, an art director, or even your own creative impulses. Dreamweaver provides a range of layout tools intended to help you adapt your designs quickly and easily. In this exercise, you'll use the ruler and guides to visually realign the content columns with a portion of a graphic.

1 If necessary, open the layout_start.html file by double-clicking its entry in the Files panel.

2 Press F4 to close any open panels and maximize your workspace.

3 Double-click the Banner image placeholder. When the Select Image Source dialog box opens, navigate to the Lessons > images folder and select bench.jpg. Click Choose.

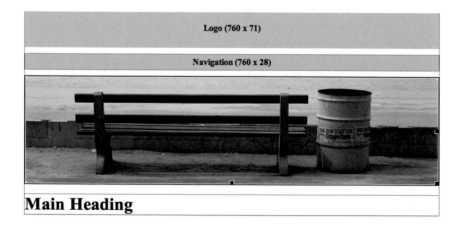

The image contains a wide bench and an eye-catching yellow barrel. A natural point between the two objects can be used as a "line" along which the text in the columns can be aligned.

As with most graphic programs, such as Adobe Photoshop or Fireworks, you'll need to display the rulers in Dreamweaver before you can use the guides.

4 Choose View > Rulers > Show, and then choose View > Rulers > Reset Origin.

You can change the origin of the ruler by dragging its upper left corner to a new location on the page. You can also double-click this corner to reset the origin to the upper left corner of the Document window.

Guides are dragged from the horizontal and vertical rulers as needed.

5 Click in the vertical ruler on the left edge of the Document window, then drag. A green guide line will appear. Drag it far enough to align it with the right edge of the bench.

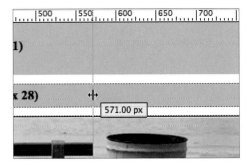

A tooltip displays the pixel distance from the ruler origin on the vertical (or Y) axis. You can adjust the position of the guide by placing your mouse pointer over the guide and, when the two-headed arrow appears, dragging it to a new location.

6 Control+drag (Windows) or Command+drag (Mac) another vertical guide from the ruler. Watch the tooltips with the pixel dimensions. Drag the guide until the two guides are 30 pixels apart. The 30 pixels will be used to create a white space between the two columns of text.

● **Note:** This exercise uses only vertical guides; horizontal guides are dragged onto the page from the horizontal ruler along the top of the Document window.

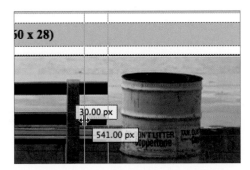

Note: To remove a guide, drag it off the page in any direction.

The dimensions displayed are from one guide to another and from the edge of the Document window. To get the exact measurements, you'll need additional guides placed on both the left and right edges of the layout.

7   Drag a vertical guide to the right edge of the layout. Notice that the guide snaps into place. Drag a final vertical guide to the left edge of the layout.

With all your guides in place, you're ready to gather the needed dimensions.

8   Place your mouse pointer between the left-most guide and the next guide, and press Control (Windows) or Command (Mac). Notice the displayed dimension, which should be 489 pixels.

9   Move your mouse pointer between the right-most guide and the next guide to the left (on the right edge of the bench). The dimension displayed here should be 241 pixels.

Now, adjust the appropriate CSS properties.

10 Choose Window > CSS Styles. If necessary, expand main.css so you can see the individual styles. In All mode, select #rightColumn, and in the Properties pane of the CSS Styles panel, double-click the current value, 365px, and type **241**. Press Enter (Windows) or Return (Mac).

11 Select #leftColumn, and in the CSS Styles Properties pane, double-click the current value, 365px, and type **489**. Press Enter (Windows) or Return (Mac).

Adjustments to the width of the two columns maintain the 30-pixel space between them while aligning them with a visual element on the page.

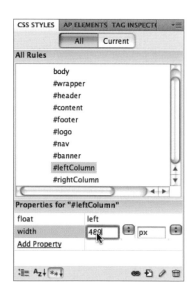

12 Choose View > Guides > Clear Guides, and then choose File > Save All. Press F4 to go to full screen mode.

You created a layout from scratch, added a number of layout <divs> to the page, and indicated with placeholder images and graphics how the completed design would look. You used guides to size columns based on the alignment of items in a graphic banner. The layout is ready to be used to create new pages and new content. Before it is used for this purpose, it's a good idea to check your work for errors. You'll do that next.

Checking the layout

Your layout has not been tested for browser compatibility or been run through a code validation check. Before you use this layout to create pages for a new site, it's a good idea to check the validity of your work.

1 If necessary, open layout_start.html in Dreamweaver.

2 Choose File > Check Page > Browser Compatibility.

When the Report box opens, there should be no issues listed.

3 To close the report, in the upper right corner of the report window, pull down the menu list and choose Close Tab Group.

4 Choose File > Validate > Markup.

When the Report box opens, you see two errors related to the quotation marks in the placeholder text for the `<div>` tags where you have phrases like *Content for id "footer" Goes Here*. Since that eventually will be removed as the page develops, ignore these errors.

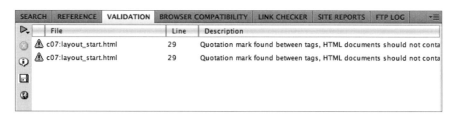

▶ **Tip:** Until you have real content on any pages using this layout, checking accessibility is unnecessary.

5 Close the window to close the report.

The layout is cross-browser compatible and has no markup errors.

You started from nothing and built a layout using `<div>` elements and CSS presentation rules that could be put into production. You duplicated and changed CSS rules, aligned the layout with rulers, learned about code navigation tools, and checked your page for browser compatibility and validity. The layout can be modified for other uses in the same ways that you have learned to modify pages using a built-in CSS Dreamweaver layout to create pages in the Here and Back Travel site.

Review questions

1 What CSS selector should you use to define zero margins and zero padding? If you want to center your layout, what property and value do you need to include in the CSS rule for backward compatibility with older browsers?

2 Name two benefits to using a #wrapper <div> tag in a CSS-based layout.

3 Describe the process for inserting a layout-styled <div> tag.

4 How do you move CSS styles from the <head> of a document to an external style sheet?

5 What's the first step to dragging a guide onto the screen?

6 What is the final step to take with a new page layout before putting it into production?

Review answers

1 Use the <body> tag as your selector; and in addition to setting margin: 0 and padding: 0, you should also set text-align: center for a centered layout.

2 A #wrapper <div> tag allows you to set the overall width for the layout in one location and to easily align the layout left, right, or center.

3 First, define the CSS layout style, typically with an ID selector, such as #header. The style can include any necessary attributes, such as margins, padding, or height. After the style is created, choose Insert Div Tag from the Layout category of the Insert panel. In the Insert Div Tag dialog box, choose where to place the <div> tag—such as after a certain other <div> tag begins, and then select the just-defined ID selector to use.

4 Use the Move CSS Styles command from the Options menu of the CSS Styles panel, which can move styles from the <head> of a document to an existing style sheet or a new sheet.

5 The first step to dragging a guide onto the screen is to display the rulers, by choosing View > Rulers > Show.

6 The page should be checked for browser compatibility and validity.

8

WORKING WITH FORMS

In this lesson, you'll create forms for your Web page and do the following:

- Insert a form

- Include text fields

- Work with Spry Form widgets

- Insert radio buttons

- Insert check boxes

- Insert lists

- Add form buttons

- Incorporate fieldsets and legends

- Style your form with CSS

 This lesson will take about 90 minutes to complete. Be sure you have copied Lessons > lesson08 from the *Adobe Dreamweaver CS4 Classroom in a Book* CD to your hard drive before beginning.

Contact Here and Back Travel

How can we help?

Contact us by phone, email, or stop by our main office in New York City.

Your Contact Information

Your Name

Your email

Online Tools

For online access to your itinerary and travel plans, please set up a username and password. *Your username must contain at least 6 characters. Your password must contain at least 8 characters, at least two of them numbers.*

Username

Password

Repeat Password

Your trip

Travel Plans

```
Briefly describe where you would like to go
and for how long
```

How many will be traveling in your group?

○ One
○ Two

Dreamweaver provides robust form solutions to help you open communication with your site visitors.

Previewing a completed file

To understand the project you will work on in this lesson, you can preview the completed page in the browser.

1 Open Dreamweaver CS4.

2 If necessary, press F8 to open the Files panel, and choose DW CIB from the site list.

3 In the Files panel, expand the lesson08 folder.

4 Select contact-finished.html, and press F12 (Windows) or Option+F12 (Mac) to preview it in your primary browser.

● **Note:** If Microsoft Internet Explorer is your primary browser and a message appears at the top of the browser window indicating that scripts are prevented from running, click the message bar and choose Allow Blocked Content.

The page includes several form elements. Try them out to observe their behaviors.

5 Click in the Your Name field and type a name. Press Tab.

The name appears in the data field.

6 Click in the "Your email" field, and then press Tab without entering an e-mail address.

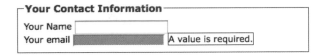

A Spry Form widget provides validation for this field and displays an error message if the field is left empty.

7 In the "Your email" field, type **jdoe@mycompany**, intentionally omitting the *.com* portion of the e-mail address. Press Tab.

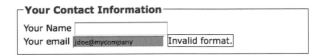

The Spry Form widget displays an error message to ensure that the information is entered in the correct format.

8 Click in the "Your email" field and type **.com** after *jdoe@mycompany*. Press Tab.

Now that the entry represents a complete e-mail address, the error message disappears.

9 Click in the Username field and type a name with fewer than six characters. Press Tab.

Another error message appears to indicate that the minimum requirements of this date field have not been met.

┌─**Online Tools**──────────────────────────────┐
│   │
│ For online access to your itinerary and travel plans, please set │
│ up a username and password. *Your username must contain at* │
│ *least 6 characters. Your password must contain at least 8* │
│ *characters, at least two of them numbers.* │
│ ─────────────────────────────── │
│ Username [jdoe   ] [Minimum number of │
│ characters not met.] │
│ Password [|] │
│ Repeat Password [   ] │
│   │
└──┘

10 Click in the Username field and type a username with six or more characters. Press Tab.

11 In the Password field, type a password with eight characters, all letters. Press Tab.

Yet another error message appears.

```
┌─Online Tools──────────────────────────────────────┐
│                                                    │
│  For online access to your itinerary and travel    │
│  plans, please set up a username and password.     │
│  *Your username must contain at least 6 characters.*│
│  *Your password must contain at least 8            │
│  characters, at least two of them numbers.*        │
│                                                    │
│  Username  [                    ]                  │
│  Password  [••••••••]  The password doesn't meet the│
│  specified strength.                               │
│  Repeat Password [                                 │
│                                                    │
└────────────────────────────────────────────────────┘
```

12 Click in the Password field and type a password with eight characters or more. At least two of the characters should be numbers. Press Tab.

13 In the Repeat Password field, type a different password than the one you typed in the Password field. Press Tab.

```
┌─Online Tools──────────────────────────────────────┐
│                                                    │
│  For online access to your itinerary and travel    │
│  plans, please set up a username and password.     │
│  *Your username must contain at least 6 characters.*│
│  *Your password must contain at least 8            │
│  characters, at least two of them numbers.*        │
│                                                    │
│  Username  [                    ]                  │
│  Password  [••••••••]                              │
│  Repeat Password [••••••••]  The values don't match.│
│                                                    │
└────────────────────────────────────────────────────┘
```

The Spry Validation Confirm widget detects that the two passwords do not match and displays an error message.

14 Return to the Repeat Password field and type a password that matches the Password field entry. Press Tab.

15 Click in the Travel Plans field and type something about a trip. Press Tab.

16 Use the radio buttons to choose a number of travelers.

17 From the Services options, select any services you'd like to request.

18 In the Timelist, choose when you plan to travel from the Timeline list.

● **Note:** No form data is actually saved in this example.

19 Click Submit to submit the form.

Note the thank-you page that appears in response.

20 When you're done, close all browser windows and return to Dreamweaver.

Before you construct your own form with its various form elements, let's take a moment to make sure you understand how forms work.

Learning about forms

Forms, on paper or on the web, gather information. In both cases, each bit of information is entered into its own data area to make it easier to understand that information. Also, the form is clearly delineated: Printed forms often use a separate page or border to distinguish them, while web forms use the <form> tag. Finally, online forms put your users to work as data-entry typists, reducing the labor costs and error rates of paper forms.

Web-based forms comprise a series of form elements, each used for a specific purpose:

- Text fields—Permit the entry of text and numbers, up to a specific number of characters. Text fields designated as password fields mask characters as they are input.

- Text areas—Identical to text fields, but intended for longer text, such as multiple sentences or paragraphs.

- Radio buttons—Permit selection of one item from a group of items. The selection of a new item in the group deselects the currently selected item.

- Check boxes—Allow a yes-or-no selection. Check boxes can be grouped together; however, unlike radio buttons, they allow multiple items to be chosen within the group.

- Lists—Display entries in a pop-up list format. Lists (also called *menus* or *select lists*) may enforce the selection of a single element or allow the choice of multiple items.

- Hidden—Convey information to the form-processing mechanism that is unseen by the user. Hidden form elements are used extensively in dynamic page applications.

- Buttons—Submit the form or perform some other single-purpose interaction, such as clearing the form.

Paper forms, when filled out, are mailed or passed along for processing. Web forms are electronically mailed or processed. The <form> tag includes an action attribute, and the value of the action attribute is triggered when the form is submitted. Often, the action is the web address for another page or server-side script that actually processes the form.

Note: The techniques for form processing are beyond the scope of this book. This lesson describes how to set up your form in preparation for processing. To learn more about dynamic applications for storing form information, see Dreamweaver Help, "Building applications visually."

Adding a form to the page

1 In the Files panel, expand the lesson08 folder, and double-click the contact-start.html file to open it.

2 Choose File > Save As. In the filename field, type **contact.html**, and click Save.

If you later want to open the original contact-start.html file, it will be preserved on your hard drive.

The `<form>` tag must surround all the form elements, so it's typically best to add it to the page first. If you try to insert a form element without a `<form>` tag, Dreamweaver will prompt you to add the `<form>` tag.

3 In the mainContent div, click after the question mark in the heading to identify the place where you want to insert your `<form>` tag.

4 In the Insert panel, choose Forms from the Category list. In the Forms category, click Form ▢.

Dreamweaver inserts the `<form>` tag at the insertion point, indicated visually with a red dashed outline.

Note: If the outline does not appear, choose Invisible Elements from the Visual Aids menu button on the Document toolbar.

How can we help you?

Next, you'll set the `<form>` tag's action attribute.

5 If necessary, choose Window > Properties to display the Properties panel. In the inspector, click the folder icon next to the Action field. In the Select File dialog box, navigate to the lesson08 folder and select form_processing.html. Click OK.

Note: You can leave the other properties at their default settings. The Method and Enctype properties depend upon the type of server-side code used to process the form data and upon the type of data submitted. As noted earlier, this server-side code would be added to the listed page as its action attribute.

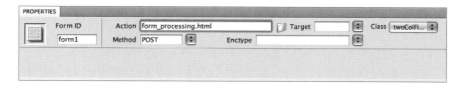

The Action field targets the page to which the form data is passed for processing. Processing can append the data to a database, create dynamic content, generate responses, or perform other actions. For this exercise, the form action merely loads the thank-you page in the browser when the form is submitted.

6 Choose File > Save.

You created the form element. Next, you'll insert form fields, starting with text fields.

Inserting text form elements

Text fields are the workhorses of all the form elements. They use an `<input>` tag and appear in the tag selector as `<input>`. Text fields are the most basic tools for gathering nonstructured data in short phrases, and it's hard to imagine a form without them. In fact, many forms are composed exclusively of text-input fields.

In the next exercises, you'll insert basic text fields, Spry Text fields, password text fields, password-confirm text fields, and text areas. Before you can start, however, confirm that Dreamweaver is configured to add form elements in their most accessible formats.

Setting preferences for accessible forms

Accessibility technologies place special requirements on form elements. Assistive technology devices, such as screen readers, require precise code that allows them to correctly read forms and individual form elements. Dreamweaver provides an option that outputs form code in the proper format. You may have set these preferences earlier; if so, merely confirm that the choices are set for accessible forms.

1. Choose Edit > Preferences (Windows) or Dreamweaver > Preferences (Mac).

2. When the Preferences dialog box appears, from the Category list choose Accessibility.

3. In the Accessibility category, make sure that the Form objects check box is selected. Click OK.

As you'll see in the following exercises, when accessibility for form objects is enabled, a dialog box appears before the form element is inserted. This dialog box has a number of options for including a form element label, as well as other special attributes. You'll learn more about these attributes later.

Using text fields

Text fields accept alphanumeric characters—letters and numbers—for a limited number of characters. The actual character limit for a text field is 255 characters, but most text fields are used for entering much shorter text strings, such as names or addresses.

1. If necessary, open the contact.html file by double-clicking its entry in the Files panel.

2. Click inside the red form outline.

3. From the Forms category of the Insert panel, choose "Text field" ⌶ .

4. In the Input Tag Accessibility Attributes dialog box, in the ID field, type **name**, and press Tab. In the Label field, type **Name** and press Tab. The `id="name"` is in lowercase, because it's code. The label *Name* begins with a capital letter, because the person filling out the form will read this label next to the form input field.

5 From the Style options, choose "Attach label tag using 'for' attribute." Make sure that in the Position options "Before form item" is selected. Click OK.

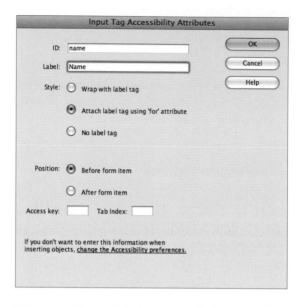

● **Note:** Text-field labels typically are placed before the field itself. As you'll see later in this lesson, radio button and check box labels are normally placed after their form fields. These conventions make forms more usable and accessible.

When the "Attach label tag using 'for' attribute" option is selected, Dreamweaver inserts code like this:

```
<label for="name">Name</label><input type="text" id="name" />
```

This code arrangement allows the `<label>` tag to be clearly connected to the form element `<input>` tag.

How can we help you?

| Name | | |

6 Choose File > Save.

The first of your form objects is now in place. Inserting other standard text fields is a similar operation. In the next exercise, you'll add a specialized version of the text field, Dreamweaver's Spry Text field.

Including Spry Text fields

In Lesson 6, you learned about Dreamweaver's Spry framework for Ajax and worked with several of the Spry tools, such as Spry Data and the Spry Accordion panel. Dreamweaver also includes a range of Spry objects for forms. Each Spry Form widget combines form elements with sophisticated JavaScript to create easy-to-use form objects with built-in *validation*.

Validation is the process of verifying that appropriate data has been entered into a form element. This maintains the integrity and quality of the data entered into the form. If a site visitor enters an incomplete or invalid e-mail address into an e-mail text field, for example, the form data might be worthless. Validation can also ensure that all required fields are completed before the form can be submitted.

Spry Form widgets are available for several kinds of form elements: text fields, text areas, check boxes, passwords, password confirmations, radio groups, and select lists. Each widget works basically the same way: You insert the widget and then adjust its properties using the Properties panel.

In this exercise, you'll insert a Spry Validation Text Field object to make sure that your form submits properly formatted e-mail addresses.

1 If necessary, open the contact.html file by double-clicking it in the Files panel.

2 Click after the previously entered Name field and press Shift+Enter (Windows) or Shift+Return (Mac) to create a line break.

3 From the Forms category of the Insert panel, choose the Spry Validation Text Field tool.

4 In the Input Tag Accessibility Attributes dialog box, in the ID field, type **email** and press Tab. In the Label field, type **Email:** and press Tab. In the Style options, make sure that "Attach label tag using 'for' attribute" is chosen. From the Position options, choose "Before form item." Click OK.

● **Note:** Each widget adds links to a JavaScript and CSS file. In these exercises, both files were copied to your hard disk in the example files from the Classroom in a Book CD. However, when you start a form on your own, Dreamweaver will notify you that these JavaScript and CSS files are being added to your site. Don't forget to upload the SpryAssets folder and the Scripts folder when the site is complete; otherwise, the widgets will not display or function properly.

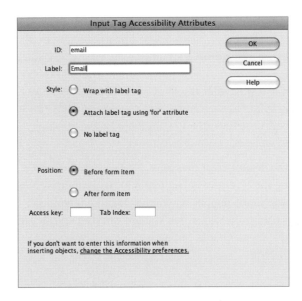

5 Choose File > Save. If Dreamweaver alerts you of the external JavaScript files used, click OK.

Now that your form element is placed on the page with the added Spry functionality, you can customize it.

6 If the Spry TextField tab isn't visible, pace your mouse pointer over the e-mail text field and wait until the Spry TextField tab appears. Click the tab to select the object.

7 If necessary, choose Window > Properties to display the Properties panel. From the Type pop-up menu, choose Email Address.

The Properties panel displays a lot of information and several adjustable attributes. As you can see, a large number of validation types are available, from Integer to Custom. The Email Address Type ensures that the entry contains an @ character followed by a domain name.

Now, set up the validation trigger.

8 In the Properties panel, choose Validate on Blur. Make sure that the Required option is chosen. When a field is required, the user must complete it before the form will submit.

By default, all validations occur when the form is submitted. In most cases, you can add more checks that take place sooner. In the current example, the field is checked for an entry with a proper e-mail format after the site visitor tabs or clicks away (on Blur) from the field. This provides a more immediate reaction and a better user experience. If the field is skipped altogether, the Required option ensures that an error message will be displayed when the form is submitted.

In this exercise, you'll accept the default error messages. However, it's easy to customize error messages using the "Preview states" menu in the Properties panel. Select any preview state and type a custom message in the Document window. To remove the error messages from your view when you are working on the page design, from the "Preview states" menu choose Initial.

Creating a fieldset

The first two text fields can be organized into a bordered box with a helpful name or phrase (called a *legend*) by using a <fieldset> tag.

1 Click to the right of the Email field, and press Enter (Windows) or Return (Mac) to create a new line.

2 Select the Name and Email labels and text fields. That can be a bit tricky in the Document window. To make sure you are selecting everything you need, click Split to use Code and Design view.

Make sure you've selected this entire code block:

```
<label for="name">Name</label>
    <input type="text" name="name" id="name" /><br />
    <span id="sprytextfield1">
    <label for="email">Email</label>
    <input type="text" name="email" id="email" />
    <span class="textfieldRequiredMsg">A value is required.
</span><span class="textfieldInvalidFormatMsg">Invalid format.
</span></span>
```

3 From the Spry category of the Insert panel, choose the Fieldset tool [⬚].

4 In the Legend field, type **Your Contact Information**. Click OK.

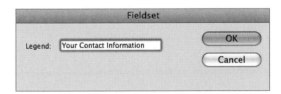

5 Choose File > Save All.

The fieldset is not easily apparent in Design view; however, you do clearly see the legend. Use Live View or a browser to preview the actual rendering of a fieldset. The fieldset neatly encloses the two fields in a labeled box.

┌─Your Contact Information───
│ Name [   ]
│ Email [   ]
└──

6 Click Live view or close your browser to return to Dreamweaver Edit mode.

Creating username and password text fields

Some text fields don't require a particular format but may require that a certain number of characters is entered. This is a common requirement in web usernames. In the next exercise, you'll add a Spry Text field to the page that has a minimum character requirement.

1 Click after the fieldset you added, but still inside the red form border, to set an insertion point. If necessary, select the fieldset and press the Right Arrow key to move past it. Press Enter (Windows) or Return (Mac) to create an empty paragraph.

2 From the Forms category of the Insert panel, choose the Spry Validation Text Field tool.

3 In the Input Tag Accessibility Attributes dialog box, in the ID field, type **username** and press Tab. In the Label field, type **Username:** and press Tab. In the Style section, ensure that the "Attach label tag using 'for' attribute" option is chosen; and, in the Position section, ensure that "Before form item" is chosen. Click OK.

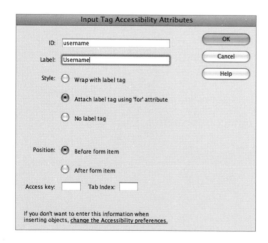

4 If necessary, place your mouse pointer over the username text field and wait until the Spry TextField tab appears. Click the tab to select the object.

5 In the Properties panel, choose Validate on Blur, and in the "Min chars" field, type **6**. Ensure that the Required check box is selected.

If the Design view displays an error message in a red background, you should go to the Properties panel and choose Preview States: Initial to remove the message from the Design view.

6 Choose File > Save.

Entering a password field

The password field is a common sight on the web. Normally, a text field displays the characters entered into it. However, when the text field is a password field, the characters entered are masked as they're typed and are depicted as a series of asterisks or bullets, depending on the browser. This is a security measure.

1 Press Shift+Enter (Windows) or Shift+Return (Mac) to create a line break after the username field.

2 From the Forms category of the Insert panel, choose the Spry Validation Password tool.

3 In the Input Tag Accessibility Attributes dialog box, in the ID field, type **password** and press Tab. In the Label field, type **Password:** and press Tab. In the Style and Position options, ensure that "Attach label tag using 'for' attribute" and "Before form item" are chosen. Click OK.

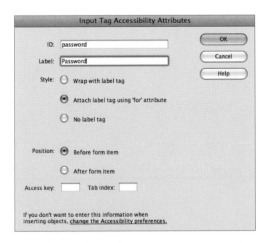

4 Click the SpryPassword tab. In the Properties panel, select "Required" and "Validate on Blur." In the "Min chars" field, type **8**. In the "Min numbers" field, type **2.**

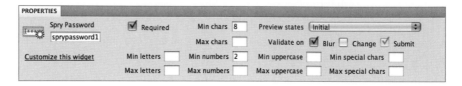

If you don't want the default error message to show in your design window, in the Properties panel, choose Preview states: Initial.

5 Press the Right Arrow key to move past the password field. Then press Shift+Enter (Windows) or Shift+Return (Mac) to create a line break after the password field.

6 In the Forms category of the Insert panel, click the Spry Validation Confirm button ☐ to create a password-confirm text field.

7 In the Input Tag Accessibility Attributes dialog box, in the ID field, type **confirmpw,** and in the Label field, type **Repeat Password**. In the Style and Position options, confirm that "Attach label tag using 'for' attribute" and "Before form item" are selected. Click OK.

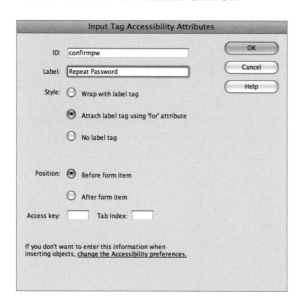

8 In the Properties panel, select Required and "Validate on Blur." From the "Validate against" pop up menu, choose "password" in form "form1."

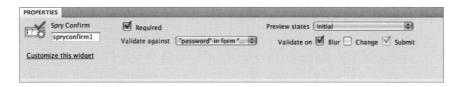

9 Click to position your mouse pointer immediately after the password-confirm field, and press Enter (Windows) or Return (Mac).

Because the website user won't know which rules apply to the username and password, an explanatory paragraph should be added prior to these three fields.

Let's move back to the empty paragraph waiting above the username field and type some instructions. If the empty paragraph is not there, select the username field, then press the Left Arrow key to move to the left of the username field and press Enter (Windows) or Return (Mac) to create it.

10 Click in the blank paragraph you created before the username field and type the following:

For online access to your itinerary and travel plans, please set up a username and password. *Your username must contain at least 6 characters. Your password must contain at least 8 characters, at least two of them numbers.*

The paragraph of instructions and the three new text fields can be enclosed in a fieldset at this point.

11 Select the paragraph and the three fields.

While you may not need to use Code view or Code and Design view to help you select the desired code this time, don't hesitate to use these valuable tools whenever necessary.

12 In the Forms category of the Insert panel, click the Fieldset button. Type **Online Tools** in the Legend field. Click OK.

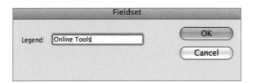

13 Choose File > Save.

The password field you added allows a website user to create a password within rules you set. The password-confirm field requires that the password be retyped in exactly the same form. This will help website users to detect typos and not accidentally submit a password that is not what they intended to type.

Incorporating text areas

Text areas allow more text to be entered than can be entered into text fields. Text areas permit multiple line entry and, by default, word wrapping. If the entered text exceeds the physical space of the text area on the page, scroll bars automatically appear.

1 If necessary, open the contact.html file by double-clicking it in the Files panel.

An alternative way to create a fieldset is to create it first and then add the form elements. You will use this method for the next few form elements.

2 Position the pointer under the last fieldset but still within the red form border. If necessary, click inside the last fieldset, then you can click <fieldset> in the tag selector and press the Right Arrow key to move past it. In the Forms category of the Insert panel, click the Fieldset button. In the Legend field, type **Your Trip** and click OK.

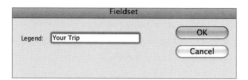

You can now enter a new form element inside the existing fieldset.

3 In the Forms category of the Insert panel, click Text Area 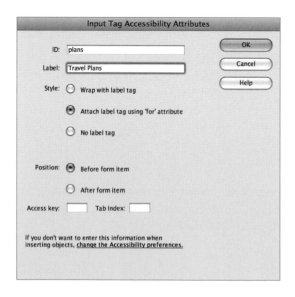.

4 In the Input Tag Accessibility Attributes dialog box, in the ID field, type **plans** and press Tab. In the Label field, type **Travel Plans**. In the Style options, ensure that "Attach label tag using 'for' attribute" is chosen; and in the Position options, choose "Before form item." Click OK.

5 The text area will appear immediately after the label. Click after the label and press Shift+Enter (Windows) or Shift+Return (Mac) to create a line break.

6 Click inside the empty text area.

It's sometimes a good idea to use the Init val field (an abbreviation for *Initial Value*) to display a helpful message to describe what is expected in a particular form element. Init val isn't always necessary, and its use depends on the label and how clear your form instructions are about what to enter in the text area.

7 Type **Briefly describe where you would like to go and for how long**.

When the website user begins to type in this field, your Initial Value hint will disappear.

● **Note:**
The Properties panel can also be used to change the width and height (Num lines) of the text area on the page. You can also set the field to be read-only (non-editable by the website user).

8 Choose File > Save.

The text area you added allows the website user to type a lengthy description (you asked for brief, but a text area easily holds several paragraphs).

Creating radio buttons

When you want people to choose one item from several items, you use radio buttons. Unlike other form elements, each radio button does not have a unique name; rather, all radio buttons in a group have the same name. To differentiate between radio buttons in a group, each is given a distinctive value.

Dreamweaver provides two methods for adding radio buttons to your page. You can either insert each radio button individually, or insert an entire group at once using the Spry Validation Radio Group widget. If you insert the radio buttons separately, you'll need to rename each of them to ensure that they all have the same name. If you add them as a Spry Validation Radio Group, they will all have the same name, and the associated JavaScript and CSS files allow customized error messages and styling. In this exercise, you'll use the widget.

1   If necessary, open the contact.html file by double-clicking it in the Files panel.

2   Click after the text-area field, but still within the fieldset with the label *Your trip*. Press Enter (Windows) or Return (Mac) to move to a new line. Type **How many will be traveling in your group?** Press Enter (Windows) or Return (Mac).

3   In the Forms category of the Insert panel, click Spry Validation Radio Group.

4   Click the Plus (+) button for Radio buttons three times to create a total of five radio buttons.

   Now you will add labels and values for these buttons.

5   Click at the top of the list, and type **One** in the Label field. Press Tab and type **one** in the Value field. Press Tab and type **Two** in the second Label field, and type **two** in the second Value field. Continue in a similar manner with the labels **Three**, **Four**, and **More**, and their respective values **three**, **four**, and **more**. From the "Lay out using" options, choose "Line breaks (
 tags)." Click OK.

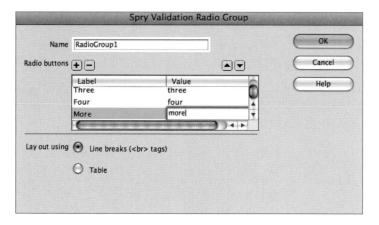

6   In the Document window, if the radio group isn't currently selected, click the blue tab to select the Spry widget for the radio group. In the Properties panel, select Required. Leave the other options set as shown in the following figure.

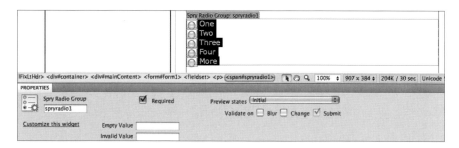

7   Choose File > Save.

You've created a set of radio buttons that allow only one choice. By using the Spry Validation Radio Group widget, you were able to make this a required form element. If the website user does not select one of the radio buttons, an error message will appear when the form is submitted.

Inserting check boxes

Check boxes provide a series of options that can be chosen in any combination. Like radio buttons, check boxes are part of a named group. Each check box has its own value and a unique ID.

1 Click after the radio button group and press Enter (Windows) or Return (Mac). In Code and Design view, you can inspect the code to be sure that you have moved beyond the closing </p> tag and the <span> that holds the error message that will appear if the required radio buttons are omitted. In Design view, type **What services would you like for us to arrange for you?** Press Enter (Windows) or Return (Mac).

Dreamweaver will insert check boxes one at a time, each time you click the check box ☑ button. Using that method, you must manually enter a group name for each check box in a set. As with radio buttons, Dreamweaver has another way to insert an entire group of check boxes with the same name. Each check box will have a distinctive label and value.

2 In the Forms category of the Insert panel, click Checkbox Group ▤.

3 In the Checkbox Group dialog box, click the Plus (+) button next to Checkboxes to create a third check box. Change the first label to **Tours** and press Tab; then, in the Value field, type **tours.** Continue until you have labels for **Transportation** and **Hotels** with their respective values, **transportation** and **hotels.** From the "Lay out using" options, choose "Line breaks (
 tags)." Click OK.

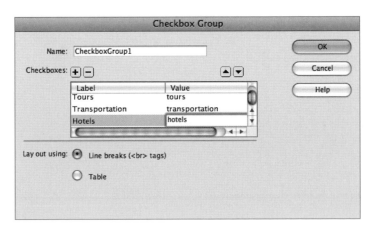

Using Checkbox Group, you don't need to set any properties in the Properties panel. A quick glance at the code reveals the value of using Checkbox Group.

Note: The generic names suggested by Dreamweaver, such as CheckboxGroup1, can be changed in the Name field in the Properties panel. For example, naming the Checkbox Group services_wanted might be more useful to you as a website owner when you looked at the submitted data from a web form. Using custom names, rather than the generic names suggested by Dreamweaver, often conveys more helpful information to the recipient of the submitted form information.

4 Click the Split button to open Code and Design view. Each check box has `name="CheckboxGroup1"` as its name.

If you enter check boxes one at a time, you must manually add the name and value for each check box. The Spry Checkbox Group saves time by automating the process.

5 Choose File > Save.

You've created a group of check boxes. By default, more than one check box can be selected in a group. As mentioned earlier in the lesson, the default position for the `<label>` with both radio buttons and check boxes is after the form element.

We have one more form element to include within the current form. Next, you'll learn how to present multiple choices in a more compact format with the list form element.

Working with lists

Pop-up list form elements are a flexible method for presenting multiple options. Typically, a list offers a single, mutually exclusive choice, like a radio button group. However, when the multiple selection option is enabled, the list behaves more like a series of check boxes. In this exercise, you'll insert a standard list with three options.

1 If necessary, open the contact.html file by double-clicking its entry in the Files panel. Click after the last check box label, and press Enter (Windows) or Return (Mac).

2 Type **When do you plan to travel?** and press Enter (Windows) or Return (Mac).

3 From the Forms category of the Insert panel, choose List/Menu 📑.

4 In the Input Tag Accessibility Attributes dialog box, in the ID field, type **timeline** and press Tab. Leave the Label field empty, in the Style options, choose "No label tag," and click OK.

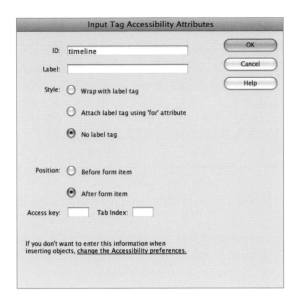

There is no need for a label tag because the text on the form element serves as label text for this form element.

Now you're ready to add the list entries. Dreamweaver provides a separate dialog box for this task, accessible in the Properties panel.

5 Select the list form element you just inserted. If necessary, choose Window > Properties. In the Properties panel, click List Values.

6 In the List Values dialog box, in the Item Label column, type **Immediately** and press Tab. Type **immediately** in the Value column. Press Tab.

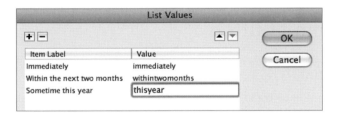

7 Complete the list as follows:

- Item Label: **Within the next two months**; Value: **withintwomonths**

- Item Label: **Sometime this year**; Value: **this year**

▶ **Tip:** You may use underscores in values names; for example, within_two_months or this_year, if you wish. Just don't use spaces in value names.

8 Click OK.

Now you'll set the list element you want displayed when the page loads; typically, this is the first item in the list.

9 In the Properties panel, from the "Initially selected" menu, choose Immediately. In the Type area, choose Menu.

When the List/Menu element is formatted with the Menu type, the list doesn't allow multiple selections. To allow users the ability to select multiple items, change the Type choice to List, and then select the "Allow multiple" check box. With a List type form element, a user can be asked, for instance, to pick her top three choices for a week of travel. After you've looked at the options for List, return to the Menu Type to finish the exercise.

10 Choose File > Save.

A menu element can contain many options—for example, all 50 states—and so adds a considerable number of choices for the website user while taking up only a small space on a web page.

Your form is almost complete—the last step is to add a button to submit all the entered information.

Adding a submit button

A submit button is needed to invoke the form action. As the name implies, this form object submits the entire form for processing and, thus, is an essential element. By default, the button object in Dreamweaver is set to submit, although other options are available. You could, for example, include a button to reset the form.

1 If necessary, open the contact.html file by double-clicking it in the Files panel.

2 Click any form element in the last fieldset. In the Properties panel, select the `<fieldset>` tag.

Next, you'll place the Submit button outside the fieldset.

3 Press the Right Arrow key to move outside the selected fieldset. Then press Enter (Windows) or Return (Mac) to create a space for the button.

4 From the Forms category of the Insert panel, choose Button 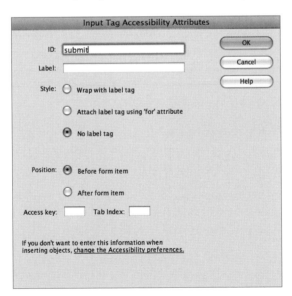.

5 In the Input Tag Accessibility Attributes dialog box, in the ID field, type **submit**. From the Style options, choose "No label tag." Click OK.

6 In the Properties panel, accept the default Action (Submit form) and the default Value (Submit). You could make the button text read something different, such as *Send* instead of *Submit*, by typing a new value in the Value field.

7 Choose File > Save.

You have completed a form that would collect names, e-mail addresses, usernames, passwords, and other information needed to make the travel arrangements for a trip. You have Spry validation scripts in place for the required fields and for other requirements, such as proper e-mail formatting or a minimum number of characters in a username. You've organized the form with fieldsets and added a Submit button. With a form-processing script linked to the Action line, this form would work as it is. But before you move on, let's add a bit of stylistic flair.

Styling forms

While the form you've been working on in this lesson is now functional, it is completely unstyled. A well-styled form has enhanced readability and comprehension, and therefore it's easier to use. In the following exercise, you'll add style to your form.

Applying CSS rules

Although a wide range of form element types is available, they share common characteristics, such as the `<label>` tag. These form elements can be styled with CSS. In this exercise, you'll create a new style sheet to contain the formatting for your form, and add rules for the legend and fieldset elements.

1 If necessary, open the contact.html file by double-clicking its entry in the Files panel.

2 Choose Window > CSS Styles.

You'll create a new style sheet just for the form styles. It will be attached to this page but needn't be attached to any other pages in the travel site. By separating the CSS rules for forms from the master style sheet, you are limiting the amount of code that must be downloaded in each page of the website, and creating a more efficient site overall. Less code means faster downloads and a better user experience. Plus, you'll gain experience in creating a new style sheet.

3 At the bottom of the CSS Styles panel, click the Attach Style Sheet button ⊕.

4 When the Attach External Style Sheet dialog box appears, in the File/URL field, type **forms.css**. From the "Add as" options, select Link, and from the Media pop-up menu, choose screen. Click OK.

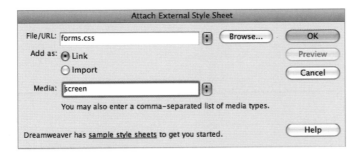

5 Dreamweaver alerts you that the named style sheet does not exist. Click Yes to link to it anyway.

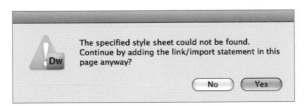

6 In the CSS panel's All Rules pane, select the forms.css listing. Then click the Plus (+) button for New CSS Rule.

7 In the New CSS Rule dialog box, from the Selector Type pop-up menu, choose "Tag (redefines an HTML element)." In the Selector Name field, type **legend,** or use the pop-up menu to select legend. In the Rule Definition section, make sure that forms.css is chosen. Click OK.

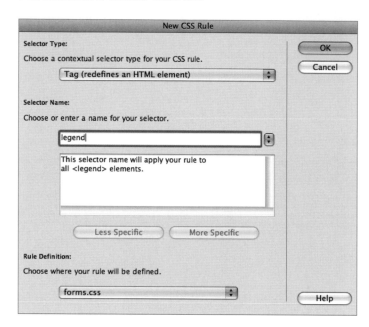

8 Dreamweaver alerts you that this style sheet does not exist and offers to create it. Click Yes.

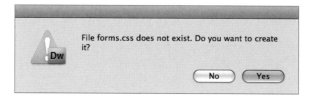

9 In the "CSS Rule Definition for legend in forms.css" dialog box, choose the Type category. In the Font-size field, type **110,** and choose **%** from the pop-up menu next to it. From the Font-weight pop-up menu, choose bold. Click the Color field and type **#345FA3**. Click OK.

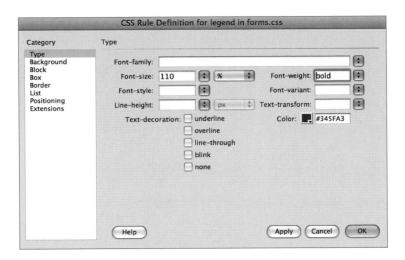

10 In the CSS Styles panel, click the Plus (+) button to add a New CSS Rule.

11 In the New CSS Rule dialog box, from the Selector Type pop-up menu, choose "Tag (redefines an HTML element)". In the Selector Name field, either type **fieldset** or choose fieldset using the pop-up menu. In the Rule Definition pop-up menu, make sure that forms.css is chosen. Click OK.

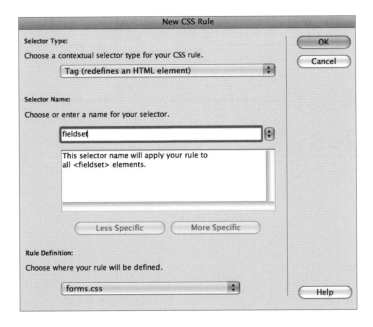

12 In the "CSS Rule Definition for fieldset in form.css" dialog box, choose the Box category. In the Padding area, type **10** in the Top field and it will propagate to all four fields. In the Margin area, deselect the "Same for all" check box and type **5** in the Bottom field. Accept the default value of px for all the measurement pop-up menus.

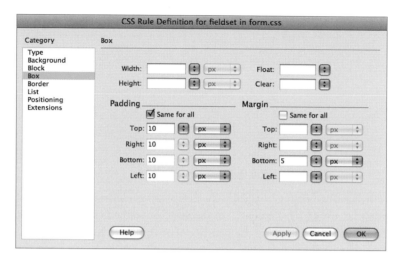

13 Choose the Border category. From the Style pop-up menus, choose solid. For Width, choose thin. For Color, type **#345FA3.** (The values will be propagated because the "Same for all" check box is selected in all areas.) Click OK.

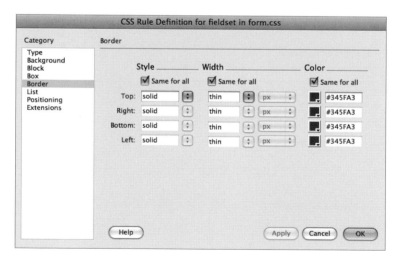

14 Choose File > Save All.

The legend and fieldset styles will appear more correctly in a rendered view of the page than in Design view.

15 Click Live View or preview the page in a browser.

16 Click Live View again, or close your browser to return to Dreamweaver's Edit mode.

SpryAssets and linked files

A considerable number of Spry scripts and style sheets are now linked to this page. Because they were already located in the SpryAssets folder to make the preview page operate, you weren't reminded to add them to your site. Remember that all the files linked to this page are listed above the Document window and need to be uploaded if the page is to work on a remote site.

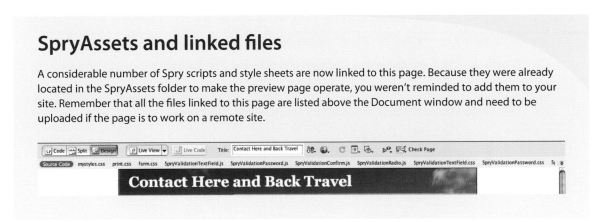

In this lesson, you built a complete form with many form elements and a number of Spry Validation widgets. You styled the form a bit to liven up its appearance and attached and created a new style sheet.

Review questions

1 What is the purpose of the `<form>` tag?

2 How do you enable the accessibility features for forms in Dreamweaver?

3 What does selecting "Attach label tag using 'for' attribute" do?

4 What advantage do the Spry Form widgets have over standard form objects?

5 What's the difference between a standard text field and a text area?

6 How do you designate that separate radio buttons belong to a group?

7 What's the main difference between radio buttons and check boxes?

8 What does a `<fieldset>` tag do?

Review answers

1 The `<form>` tag wraps around all the form elements and includes an action attribute that defines the file or script to handle the form processing.

2 In Dreamweaver Preferences, under the Accessibility category, select Form Objects.

3 It connects the `<label>` tag to the form element, which has a matching ID value.

4 Spry Form widgets make it easier to create form elements such as radio buttons and check boxes. They include built-in validation to ensure that the data submitted is properly formed and, if required, is completed.

5 A standard text field is intended for short character strings, while a text area can hold multiple paragraphs.

6 All radio buttons with the same name will be in the same radio button group.

7 Radio buttons only allow for mutually exclusive choices, while check boxes permit the user to select as many items as desired.

8 A `<fieldset>` tag is used to group related form fields within a border; the accompanying `<legend>` tag identifies the group. It helps organize a form and clarify the purpose of the various form fields.

9 WORKING WITH FLASH

In this lesson, you'll incorporate Flash into your web page and do the following:

- Insert a Flash movie

- Add a Flash video

 This lesson will take about 30 minutes to complete. Be sure you have copied Lessons > lesson09, Lessons > movie, and Lessons > Scripts from the *Adobe Dreamweaver CS4 Classroom in a Book* CD to your hard drive before beginning.

Here and Back Travel

Boston's beautiful Realty Park can be on your itinerary

Have the vacation of a lifetime
with Here and Back Travel

Welcome to Here and Back Travel, home of the personalized itinerary and the best in individual attention to your travel needs.

Pick a destination and we'll make it happen, just the way you dreamed it!

Here and Back Travel
Contact Us

Dreamweaver adds Flash videos and movies
to a web page with just a few easy steps.

Previewing a completed file

To see what you will work on in the first part of this lesson, preview the completed page in the browser. This page is the home page of the travel site you've assembled in the other lessons.

1   Open Adobe Dreamweaver CS4.

2   If necessary, press F8 to open the Files panel, and choose DW CIB from the site list.

3   In the Files panel, expand the lesson09 folder.

● **Note:** Some versions of Microsoft Internet Explorer may ask you to give permission to run active content in order to play the movie. If your Flash player is not the latest version, you may be asked to download a new version.

4   Select the index-finished.html file, and press F12 (Windows) or Option+F12 (Mac) to preview it in your primary browser.

The page includes two Flash elements.

5   Note that the Flash movie plays immediately when the page loads.

6   Move your pointer over the video in the left column, and click Play to watch the Flash video.

You'll notice that if you move your pointer away from the video, the controls fade, but they return when your pointer is positioned over the video.

7   When you're done, close your browser and return to Dreamweaver.

Adding a Flash movie to a page

Adobe Flash is defined by its multimedia functions. From its humble beginnings as an animation program, Flash has rapidly grown to handle top-line advertisements, user interfaces, and even video. As befits this versatile authoring tool, the Flash Player—the tool required to play Flash's SWF files—enjoys the widest distribution of any browser plug-in.

Dreamweaver seamlessly integrates with Flash movies. SWF files can be easily inserted and previewed in the Document window. Moreover, key properties, such as Autoplay and Loop, are quickly modified in the Properties panel. If the Flash movie source file is available, you can edit the SWF file in Flash and automatically export it to Dreamweaver.

In this exercise, you'll insert a Flash movie into the mainContent area of your web page.

1 In the Files panel, expand the lesson09 folder, and double-click the index-start. html file to open it.

2 Choose File > Save As. Save the file to the lesson09 folder as *index.html*. Most websites use *index.html* for the home page filename. This page is the travel site home page.

Dreamweaver's placeholder-image capabilities can reserve space for the Flash elements inserted during this lesson.

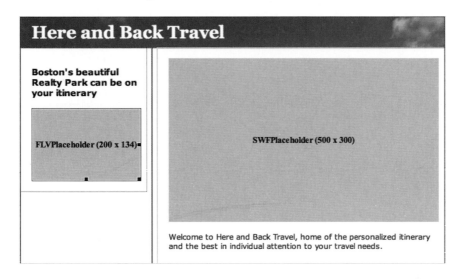

3 Select the placeholder image SWFPlaceholder and press Delete. A SWF file is not an image; the placeholder merely kept the space open.

4 Choose Insert > Media > SWF.

5 When the Select File dialog box appears, navigate to the movie folder and select hereandback.swf. Click OK (Windows) or Choose (Mac).

6 In the Object Tag Accessibility Attributes dialog box, in the Title field, type **Have a great vacation with Here and Back Travel**. Click OK.

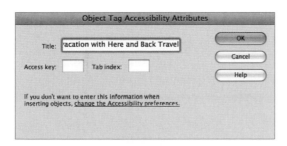

● **Note:** You have already copied the Scripts folder from the Dreamweaver Classroom in a Book CD to your hard drive. When you insert a Flash file onto a fresh page, you normally see a message explaining that the dependent files swffix_modified.js and expressInstall.swf will be placed into the Scripts folder. To make a movie play on a live website, the Scripts folder must be uploaded to the server along with the HTML files and the movie folder. The SWF files for the movie are already available in the lesson09 folder, and these files would also be uploaded to the server if the site were live.

Dreamweaver inserts the Flash code, represented in Design view by a placeholder element. You can preview your newly inserted Flash movie right in Dreamweaver.

7 If necessary, choose Window > Properties. In the Properties panel, click Play to preview the movie in Dreamweaver.

● **Note:** This SWF file is not meant to loop and was created to run only once. Some movies will loop, if desired, and can be set to do so using the Loop option in the Properties panel. Loop may be selected by default in your Properties panel. It's harmless to leave it selected, but the movie in this exercise will not loop.

Make sure that Autoplay is selected in the Properties panel so that the movie will play automatically when the page loads into the browser.

8 Choose File > Save to save your work.

Code in the page can ensure that viewers are using the latest version of the Flash Player.

9 Click the Code button to view the code. Find this block of code:

```
<!-- The browser displays the following alternative content
for users with Flash Player 6.0 and older. -->

<div><h4>Content on this page requires a newer version of
Adobe Flash Player.</h4>

<p><a href="http://www.adobe.com/go/getflashplayer"><img
src="http://www.adobe.com/images/shared/download_buttons/
get_flash_player.gif" alt="Get Adobe Flash player" /></a>
</p></div>
```

If a website user visits your site using a Flash Player older than version 6.0, she will see the message set in this block of code instead of viewing the Flash movie. You can edit this message in Code view. The website user can follow the link to the Adobe download page to acquire the latest Flash Player.

10 Click Design to return to Design view.

You've added a Flash file in SWF format to a web page. SWF files can be used for something large, as in this example, or something quite small, such as a menu button or heading text. An SWF file is created in Adobe Flash CS4 and is quickly added to a web page using the Dreamweaver Insert menu.

Flash embedding

From a Dreamweaver user's perspective, Flash is inserted into Dreamweaver CS4 much as it was inserted in previous versions. However, Dreamweaver CS4 has made significant code changes for Flash embedding. As a result, Dreamweaver CS4 is now in compliance with web standards for `<object>` elements. The code changes include the following:

- The proprietary embed elements and active content scripts used previously are gone. Instead, a `<script>` tag points to two dependent files.
- The `<object>` tag is used instead of the `<embed>` tag.
- An in-place Flash Player installation is implemented using Express Installer.
- Alternate content appears if the Flash Player is missing or is an incorrect version.

For further information, visit www.alistapart.com/articles/flashembedcagematch/.

Adding Flash video to a page

Because the Flash Player was available in almost all browsers, the introduction of Flash video was revolutionary. Overnight, all the hassle and confusion over incompatible video formats and players vanished. With recent releases of the Flash Player, the video quality has increased, along with its ubiquity. Flash video is now the leading video format on the web.

Video from cameras, phones, and other portable devices can be converted to FLV files using the Adobe Flash CS4 Video Encoder. A native Flash video file has an FLV file extension and can be played in one of two ways:

- Progressive Download—Video begins playing after a brief delay during which the first segment is received by the browser. The video continues to download during playback. Progressive download FLV files can be hosted on any standard web server.

- Streaming—Video starts playing immediately and offers advantages over progressive download such as *seekability*, which means the video playhead can be moved to any position to instantly begin playing at that point. However, streaming FLV files must be hosted on a specialized web server such as Flash Media Server.

In this exercise, you'll place an FLV in progressive download format on your page.

1 If necessary, open the index.html file by double-clicking its entry in the Files panel.

2 Select the image placeholder FLVPlaceholder, and press Delete.

3 Choose Insert > Media > FLV.

4 When the Insert FLV dialog box appears, make sure the Video Type pop-up menu is set to Progressive Download Video. Click Browse and navigate to the movie folder. Choose realty_park.flv, and click Choose. From the Skin pop-up menu, choose Corona Skin 2. Select the Constrain check box. In the Width field, type **200**, and in the Height field type **134**. Click OK.

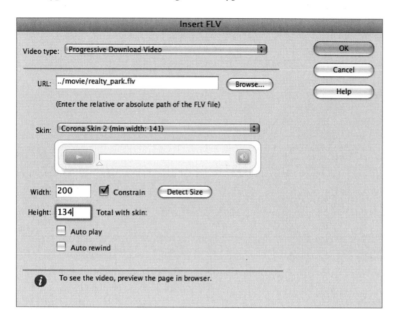

The Corona Skin 2 will fit the width you are limited to in the sidebar, and it appears and disappears when the website user moves the pointer over the video.

As with the SWF file, Dreamweaver inserts a placeholder, which can be customized with the Properties panel. Unlike Flash movies, however, Flash video cannot be previewed within Dreamweaver and must be viewed in a browser.

● **Note:** Scripts associated with the Flash Player are already in your Scripts folder. If you were creating a new page, you would be notified of the dependent files needed to enable the Flash Player.

5 Choose File > Save. Click Live View, or press F12 (Windows) or Option+F12 (Mac) to preview the page in your primary browser. If the video controls are not visible, move your pointer over the still image to display the player controls. Click Play to verify that the movie is working correctly. Click the speaker button to turn the sound off and on. When you're done, click Live View, or close your browser and return to Dreamweaver.

You've added a Flash video with a skin that allows the user to start and stop the video, and to turn the sound off and on. You also constrained the size of the video to fit within the limited space on the sidebar.

Review questions

1 What performance difference exists between the two types of Flash, SWF and FLV?

2 Identify two Flash video formats. Which format does not require a specialized web server?

3 When will a website user see the alternative content?

Review answers

1 A SWF file plays automatically with no controllers. An FLV file includes controllers for playback and sound.

2 The two Flash video formats are progressive download and streaming. Progressive download files do not require a specialized server, while streaming files do.

3 Alternative content will display if the user does not have Flash Player, or if his version of Flash Player is outdated.

10 INCREASING PRODUCTIVITY

In this lesson, you'll learn how to work faster, make updating easier, and be more productive. You'll use Dreamweaver templates, Library items, and server-side includes to do the following:

- Create a template
- Insert editable regions
- Produce child pages
- Update templates and child pages
- Create, insert, and update Library items
- Create, insert, and update server-side includes

 This lesson will take about 60 minutes to complete. Be sure you have copied Lessons > lesson10 from the *Adobe Dreamweaver CS4 Classroom in a Book* CD to your hard drive before beginning.

Here and Back Travel

Home

Italy ▸

Greece ▸

About Us ▸

Boston's beautiful Realty Park can be on your itinerary

Have the vacation of a lifetime

with Here and Back Travel

Welcome to Here and Back Travel, home of the personalized itinerary and the best in individual attention to your travel needs.

Pick a destination and we'll make it happen, just the way you dreamed it!

Dreamweaver's productivity and site management capabilities are among its most useful features for a busy designer.

Previewing completed files

To preview a completed page that you will work on in this lesson, view it in a browser. You won't be able to preview the behind-the-scenes techniques that save time and work while making the completed site, but you will understand the goal of these exercises.

1 Open Adobe Dreamweaver CS4.

2 If necessary, press F8 to open the Files panel, and choose DW CIB from the site list.

3 In the Files panel, expand the lesson10 folder.

4 Select the index-finished.html file and press F12 (Windows) or Option+F12 (Mac) to preview it in your primary browser.

   You will bring every page in the site to its completed state during this lesson by adding the menu bar.

5 Close your browser and return to Dreamweaver.

Creating a template

A Dreamweaver template is a type of master page from which child pages are derived. Templates are useful for setting up a master page in which some areas are editable and others are not. When working in team environments, page content can be changed by several people on the team, while the web designer is able to control the page design and specific elements that must remain unchanged.

Although you can create a template from a blank page, it is far more practical—and common—to convert an existing page into a template. In this exercise, you'll create a template from an existing page.

1 Open Dreamweaver.

2 If necessary, press F8 to open the Files panel, and choose DW CIB from the site list.

3 In the Files panel, expand the lesson10 folder and double-click the template-start.html file to open it.

   The basic operation for converting an existing page to a template is a single step: You save the page as a template.

4 Choose File > Save as Template.

   Because of their special nature, templates are stored in their own folder, Templates, which Dreamweaver creates at the site root level.

5 When the Save As Template dialog box appears, make sure that DW CIB is chosen in the Site pop-up menu. In the "Save as" field, type **hereandback**, and leave the Description field empty. (If you use more than one template in a site, a description may be useful.) Click Save. When Dreamweaver asks if you'd like to update links, click Yes.

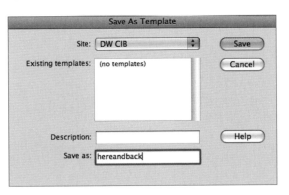

● **Note:** Because the new template is stored in a different location than the file from which it was derived, it's important to update links to any images, CSS style sheets, or other dependent files.

Although the page still looks exactly the same, you can identify a template in the title bar, which now has the added term: <<Template>>. Additionally, the file extension is *.dwt*, indicating a Dreamweaver template.

Inserting editable regions

When you create a template, Dreamweaver treats all the existing content as part of the master design and allows you to edit it only when the template file is open. Child pages created from the template would be exact duplicates; however, the content would locked and uneditable. This is acceptable for repetitive features of a page, such as the navigation components, logos, contact information, and so on, but it stops you from adding unique content to the page at first. You get around this barrier by defining "editable regions" in your template. In fact, an advantage to using templates is related to the multiple region types that can be defined in them. One editable region is automatically inserted around the <title> element in the <head> section of the page, while others must be created manually.

1   If necessary, in the Files panel, expand the Templates folder and double-click the hereandback.dwt file to open it.

You can also access your templates from the Templates category of the Assets folder.

2   Click to position your pointer in the <div> for mainContent.

3   Choose Insert > Template Objects > Editable Region.

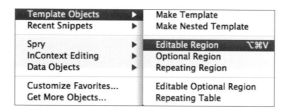

4   In the New Editable Region dialog box, type **mainContent** in the Name field. Click OK.

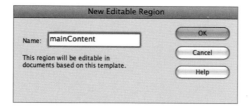

Each editable region must have a unique name. These names are displayed in the tab, which—along with the border—identifies an editable region. Some placeholder text is also present: *mainContent*.

Although it's not necessary, it's nice to replace the placeholder text with something a little more helpful to the user.

5 Select the content within the new editable region, and type **Heading**. Use the Properties panel to change this to a heading 2. Press Enter (Windows) or Return (Mac), and type **Content and images go here**.

When creating a child page from this template, these placeholder reminders will help anyone who adds actual content in a new page to understand the purpose of the editable region.

6 Click under the menu bar in the Sidebar area to set an insertion point.

7 Choose Insert > Template Objects > Editable Region.

8 In the New Editable Region dialog box, type **sidebarContent** as the region name. Click OK.

9 Select the placeholder text in the sidebarContent region and type **Content and images for the sidebar go here.**

To allow each page to have a unique name in its header area, you can add an editable region for that, too.

10 In the header area, position your mouse pointer in the text *Here and Back Travel*. Use the Tag selector to select the <h1> tag so that the entire element is included in the editable region.

11 Choose Insert > Template Objects > Editable Region.

12 In the New Editable Region dialog box, type **pageName** as the region name. Click OK. Choose File > Save.

Now the page header can be changed for each new page.

You now have three editable regions, plus an editable title, that can be changed as needed when you create new child pages using this template. The template is linked to your style sheets and other dependent files, so any changes in those files will be reflected in all child pages made from this template.

Updating a template

Changes to the template will automatically update any child pages made from that template. If you plan to use templates, it makes sense to include the menu bar as part of the template to enable global changes to the menu. Let's change the menu now to learn how a template is updated.

1 In the Document window, click the Spry Menu Bar: MenuBar1 to select the menu.

2 In the Properties panel for MenuBar1, select About Us. Above the second column, click the Plus (+) button to add a new menu item.

3 In the Properties panel Text field, select "Untitled item" and type **Our Clients**. Next to the Link field, click the Folder icon to browse for the file. Locate lesson10 > ourclients.html and click OK (Windows) or Choose (Mac).

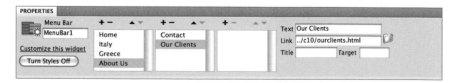

4 Choose File > Save.

5 Choose File > Close.

You've created a template, added editable regions, and updated the template with a new item in the menu bar.

Producing child pages

Child pages are the *raison d'être* for Dreamweaver templates. Once a child page has been created from a template, the content within the editable regions can be updated while the rest of the page remains locked. However, this ability is only noticeable within Dreamweaver. After a child page is published or previewed, it appears just like any other HTML page.

The decision to use Dreamweaver templates for a site should be made at the beginning of the design process, so that all the pages in the site can be made as child pages of the template. Instead of retrofitting the existing pages of the Here and Back Travel site you've been building, you'll create a single example page from the template.

1 Choose File > New.

2 In the New Document dialog box, select Page from Template from the category list on the left. Make sure that DW CIB is selected in the Site list, and that hereandback is selected in the "Template for Site 'DW CIB'" list.

3 Select the "Update page when template changes" check box, if necessary. Click Create.

The new page opens in Dreamweaver. Before modifying the page, you should save it.

4 Choose File > Save. In the Save As dialog box, navigate to the lesson10 folder, and in the "File name" field, type **template-exercise.html**; click Save.

Move your pointer around the page. Certain areas, such as the menu bar and footer, are locked and cannot be modified. The locked state is indicated as the pointer changes to the international symbol for no entry, a red circle with a diagonal line through it. The editable region content, however, can be changed.

5 In the Title field of the Document toolbar, click before Here and Back Travel. Type **Test Page:** and press Enter (Windows) or Return (Mac).

Title: Test Page: Here and Back Trave

● **Note:** When you update and save a template from which child pages have been created, Dreamweaver asks if you want to update pages that were made from the template. Approve the update, and all your child pages will be updated automatically. You may want to choose "Don't Update" at times and update the child pages later. This is useful if you have numerous changes to make and only want to run the update when you're finished. Keep in mind that any pages changed by a template update will have to be uploaded to the server to make the changes appear on a live website.

▶ **Tip:** Alternatively, select a template in the Template category of the Assets panel, Right-click (Windows) or Control-click (Mac) and choose "New from Template"

6 In the pageName editable region, select the text and type **Test Page.**

7 In the mainContent region, select Heading and type **Beautiful New Page**.

8 In the Files panel, double-click vacation.txt to open it. Select all the text and Choose Edit > Copy. Then choose File > Close.

9 In the template-exercise.html page, select the text under the heading and choose Edit > Paste to insert the content.

> **mainContent**
> ## Beautiful New Page
>
> Come enjoy the vacation of a lifetime! We do the work and you have the fun! Our tour through the hill towns of Umbria is unequalled. For two weeks, you'll enjoy worry free pampering.
>
> Every day, a delicious breakfast and dinner (with wine) are included. Lunch is on your own. Travel in air conditioned buses on ten wonderful day trips to the surrounding beautiful, historic hill towns.
>
> Our luxury hotel accommodations include a hot tub, pool, and nearby by night time entertainment. Your weekend is free to schedule as you wish, but your meals are always provided by our excellent chefs.

10 Select the text in the sidebarContent area. In the Common category of the Insert panel, select Image from the Images menu. In the Select Image Source dialog box, navigate to the images folder and select city.jpg. Click Choose.

11 In the Image Tag Accessibility Attributes dialog box, type **city view** in the Alternative text field. Click OK.

12 Choose File > Save.

13 Click Live View or preview the page in a browser.

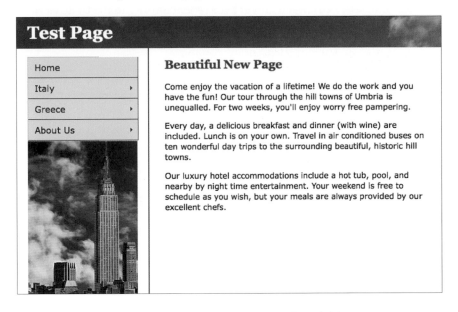

As you can see, there is no indication that this template child page is any different from any other standard web page. You can enter any content you want in the editable regions: text, images, tables, Flash video, and so on.

14 Click Live View or close the browser to return to Dreamweaver. Choose File > Close.

Using Library items

Library items are reusable bits of HTML—paragraphs, links, copyright notices, navigation bars, tables, images—that you use frequently within a website. You can use an existing page element or create original Library items and add copies of them where needed. When you update a Library item, Dreamweaver updates every page that uses that item. In seconds, the pages are updated, and those updated pages can be uploaded to the server for display on a live website.

Creating a Library item

In this exercise, you'll make the site menu into a Library item and add the Library item to every page in the site.

1 In the Files panel, expand the lesson10 folder and double-click naxos.html to open it.

2 Click the Split button so that you can see the Code and Design view while you work.

3 In the Document window, insert your mouse pointer in MenuBar1. Use the tag selector to select `<ul.MenuBarVertical#MenuBar1>`. In the Code view, verify that everything from the opening `<ul>` tag to the closing `</ul>` tag of the menu bar is included in the selection.

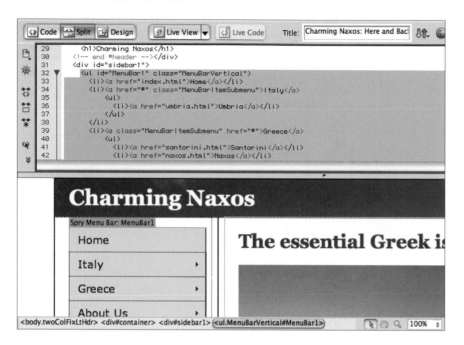

4 Choose Modify > Library > Add Object to Library. A warning appears: "This selection may not look the same when placed in other documents because the Style Sheet information is not copied with it." Click OK.

Dreamweaver adds a folder at the site root level called Library where Library items are stored. You do not need to upload this folder to the server.

You work with Library items in the Assets panel.

● **Note:** Items are stored in the Library as HTML code. Separated from its CSS formatting, the menu appears unstyled in the Assets panel. But don't worry. When the item is inserted into a page attached to the appropriate style sheet, the styling will reappear.

5 If necessary, choose Window > Assets. When the Assets panel opens, type **menubar** as the name for the new Library item.

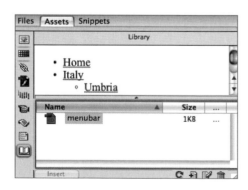

6 An Update Files dialog box appears. Click Update.

In the Document window Code view, look for the new Library item tags that now enclose the list making up the menu bar. The opening tag is

```
<!-- #BeginLibraryItem "/Library/menubar.lbi" -->
```

The closing tag is

```
<!-- #EndLibraryItem -->
```

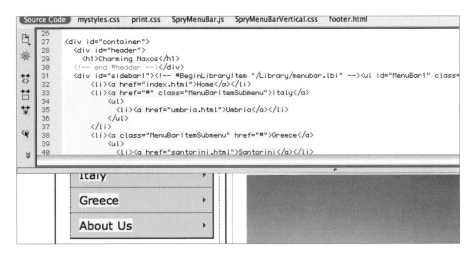

Inserting a Library item

Library items can be inserted anywhere in a page. They save time and work because the same code can be reused in a number of places, and all of it can be updated in one operation.

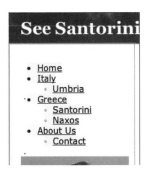

1 In the Files panel, expand the lesson10 folder and double-click santorini.html to open it.

2 Click to the left of the image of the man and woman at the top of the sidebar.

3 In the Assets panel, select the Library item, menubar, and at the bottom left of the Assets panel window, click the Insert button.

The menu appears as the unstyled list. Note the yellow background, a visual indication of a Library item.

You've inserted a Library item into a page.

If the Library item were text—perhaps a copyright notice, or an image such as a logo—you would be finished with the process. However, this particular Library item is a Spry widget. For that reason, you'll need to take extra steps that normally would not apply to a Library item that wasn't based on a Spry widget.

Linking to the dependent files

As you know, Spry widgets won't work unless linked to a CSS file and a JavaScript file stored in the SpryAssets folder. Spry widgets need a third element as well. At the bottom of the page in which you originally created the SpryMenuBar (naxos.html), a block of code is present that isn't present on the santorini.html page. In this exercise, you'll make all that work with the Library item.

1 While working with santorini.html open, in the CSS Styles panel, click the link icon for Attach Style Sheet ⏚.

2 When the Select Style Sheet File dialog box appears, click Browse. In the Select Style Sheet File dialog box, select SpryAssets > SpryMenuBarVertical.css. Click Choose.

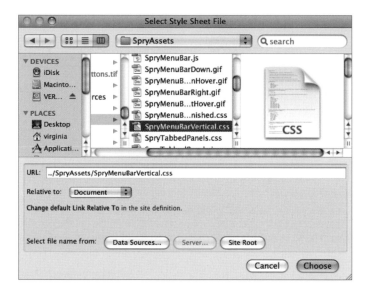

3 In the Attach External Style Sheet dialog box, choose Link from the "Add as" options, and from the Media pop-up menu, choose screen. Click OK.

The menu appears styled in the Design view but isn't functional yet.

4 If necessary, click Split to see the Code and Design view. Scroll in the Code view to find the `<script>` and `<link>` tags in the document `<head>`. Click to position an insertion point after the last `<script>` tag you see.

5 Press Enter (Windows) or Return (Mac) to create a new line at the insertion point.

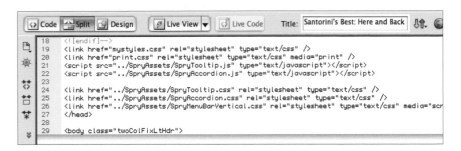

6 Choose Insert > HTML > Script Objects > Script.

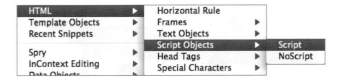

7 A Script dialog box appears. Click the folder icon to browse for the file.

8 In the Select File dialog box, choose SpryAssets > SpryMenuBar.js. Click Choose.

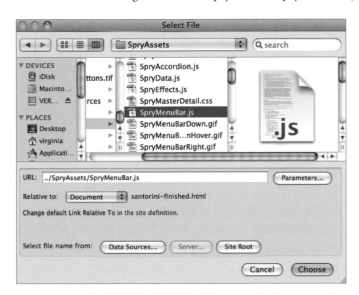

9 Click OK to close the Script dialog box.

▶ **Tip:** It's a good practice to store a site's JavaScript files externally. When linking a script to a page, as in these steps, it's important to insert the script link in the document `<head>`.

10 The new script tag appears in the `<head>` at the insertion point.

Don't worry that the `type` attribute is first and the `scr` attribute is second, unlike the other script tags. Attribute order doesn't affect function.

11 Choose File > Save.

You've linked the two dependent files that operate the Spry widget to the page. Each time you add the menubar Library item to a new page, you'll have to repeat these steps. If the Library item is something other than a Spry widget—perhaps a site description in the header or a privacy notice in the footer—linking to dependent files is not necessary.

One more step remains to make the Spry widget work in a Library item. Before you change the Library item, you can add it to every page.

Adding the menu

Several pages in the Here and Back Travel site still lack a menu. Use the following steps to complete the site navigation.

1 In the Files panel, find the lesson10 folder. Double-click contact.html to open it.

2 Click before any content in the sidebar to set an insertion point.

3 Click the Assets panel tab. If necessary, click the book icon on the left side of the Assets panel to reveal the Library items.

4 Select the menubar Library item. At the bottom left of the Assets panel, click the Insert button.

5 For many types of Library items, step 4 would end the process of adding the item to the page. But it is not sufficient for a Library item that adds a Spry widget. Repeat the steps in the section, "Linking to the dependent files" to add links to SpryMenuBarVertical.css and SpryMenuBar.js to the `<head>` of the page.

6 Repeat steps 2–5 for the files form_processing.html, index.html, ourclients.html, and umbria.html. If no `<script>` elements are present in the document head, as you find in form_processing.html, then insert the new `<script>` element after the last `<link>` element for the style sheets.

Updating Library items

Templates, Library items, and the server-side includes exist for one reason: to make it easy to update web page content. Let's update the menubar Library item.

1 If necessary, in the lesson10 folder, double-click naxos.html to open it.

   Spry widgets need the CSS and JavaScript dependent files you've worked with since Lesson 3, but they also need a third element, a block of code called the *JavaScript operator*. It's normally added at the very end of a page, but for the purposes of this exercise (and to make the menu work on the pages where you added it), you will move this code block into the Library item.

2 Click the Code button to view the code.

3 Scroll to the end of the page. At approximately lines 83–87 you will see a `<script>` block.

4 Select the entire block from the opening `<script>` tag to the closing `</script>` tag.

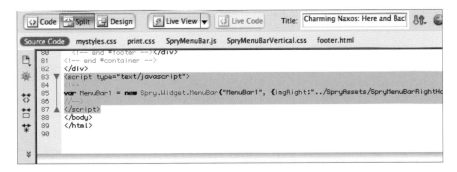

5 Choose Edit > Cut to remove the text from the page and store it in the Clipboard.

6 Click Design to return to Design view.

7 In the Document window, select the menubar Library item.

8 In the Properties panel for the Library item, click Open.

   When you open and edit a Library item in the Properties panel, you are editing every Library item on every page in the site, too.

9 When the Library item opens, click the Code button to view the code.

10 Find the last line of code, and click there to set an insertion point.

11 Choose Edit > Paste to paste the code block into the Library item.

12 Choose File > Save. In the Update Library Items dialog box, click Update. Dreamweaver will look through the files that use the Library item menubar and notify you when the updates are finished. Click Close.

13 Click the X in the menubar.lbi tab, or choose File > Close to close the Library item. Any copies of the Library item that have been added to any pages in the site will automatically reflect your change. The menubar Library item should work properly on every page in which it was inserted.

14 In the Files panel, select the index.html file and press F12 (Windows) or Option+F12 (Mac) to preview it in your primary browser.

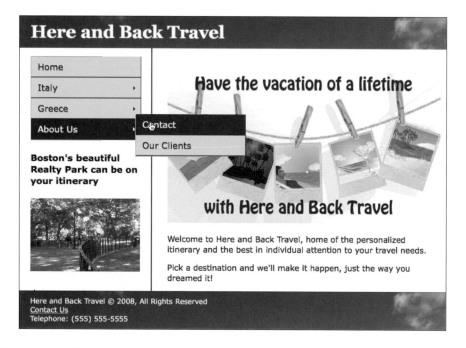

15 Navigate the entire site using the menu bar to move from page to page.

16 Close the browser and return to Dreamweaver.

You've completed updates to the entire site using Library items. You can see that the ability to quickly update pages using Library items and templates can save you a lot of time when working with a large site. And Dreamweaver still has one more trick up its productivity sleeve: server-side includes.

Using server-side includes

Server-side includes are like Library items in some ways. They are reusable bits of HTML—paragraphs, links, copyright notices, navigation bars, tables, images, and so on—that you use frequently. You create the file to include and add an include command to a page, which inserts the HTML snippet where indicated. It all happens *on the server*, which is the key difference between templates, Library items, and server-side includes. A server-side include goes on the server and is inserted in the page on the server. If you change a server-side include, you don't have to upload the pages that use it; you just upload the one file to be included.

In terms of productivity, server-side includes are the most efficient and timesaving way to add reusable HTML snippets to a large number of pages. They are faster and easier to work with than either Templates or Library items. Only one file (the include file) must be maintained, and only one upload made when the file is changed.

In this exercise, you will create an include file and add it to all the pages in your site.

▶ **Tip:** Most servers work with server-side includes, but the requirements for making them may vary from server to server. Be sure to read the instructions provided by your hosting company so that you can properly create server-side includes for your server.

Creating server-side includes

A server-side include is HTML, although everything is removed except the snippet that makes up the include.

1 Choose File > New. Select Blank Page; then, from the Page Type list, choose HTML, and from the Layout list, choose <none>. Click Create.

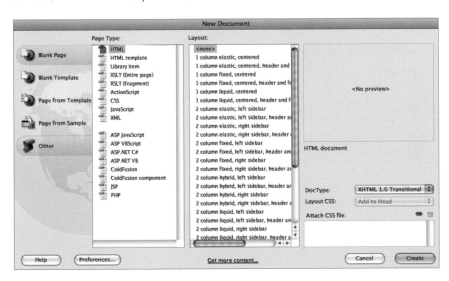

2 Leave the blank document open. In the Files panel, expand the lesson10 folder and double-click naxos.html to open it.

3 In the footer, click within the text. In the Tag selector, choose the <p> tag to make sure you select all of the code. Choose Edit > Copy. Leave this page open.

4 Click the tab for the untitled document to return to the new blank page.

5 Choose Edit > Paste.

This text would be adequate for creating the include, but you can add something before you save it to distinguish it from the previous text in the footer, so you'll see a difference when you add it.

6 Click to set an insertion point after the word *Travel*.

7 In the Text category of the Insert panel, from the Characters pop-up menu, choose Copyright.

The copyright symbol appears in your document.

8 Following the copyright symbol, type a space and type **2008, All Rights Reserved**. (Or use the current year.)

It's especially important to make sure that no <html> or <body> tags remain in the code. Remember, this isn't a page; it's merely a snippet that will be included in a page.

9 Click the Split button to see Code and Design view. In the Code view, delete all the page elements except the two lines of text that appear in the Design view.

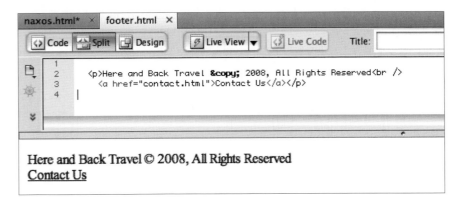

10 Choose File > Save. In the Save As field, type **footer.html**. Be sure that you are saving the file in the prepared lesson10 > includes folder. Click Save.

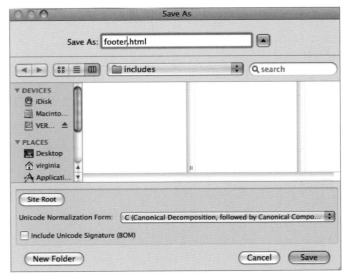

● **Note:** In a real-world situation, the includes folder probably would be located at the site's root rather than in a subfolder, as in this exercise.

11 Choose File > Close. Leave the file naxos.html open for the next exercise.

Inserting server-side includes

On a live website, you would upload the include folder to the server along with any HTML snippets it contained. A simple include command in the code of any page on your site would make a *call* to the server to add the HTML snippet in the indicated location. The include command looks like this:

```
<!--#include file="includes/footer.html" -->
```

You can see that it consists of an include command and a link to the file that will be included. Some variations may exist in include commands, depending on whether you are using an Apache- or a Windows-based server, and which file extension you use for the include file. In this exercise, you're using *.html*, but *.inc*, *.txt*, and *.shtml* are also common.

Before you begin, make sure that Dreamweaver's Preferences are set to show the included file in Design view.

1   Choose Edit > Preferences (Windows) or Dreamweaver > Preferences (Mac).

2   From the Category list, choose Invisible Elements. Be sure the Show Contents of Included File option for "Server-Side includes" is selected. Click OK.

▶ **Tip:** Many modern home computers can be set up as a testing server that will render server-side includes for testing purposes. For more information about setting up a testing server, see the Dreamweaver Help files or visit http://help. adobe.com/en_US/ Dreamweaver/10.0_ Using/. Click to expand the topics "Working with Dreamweaver sites" > "Setting up a Dreamweaver site" and read the page called "Set up a testing server."

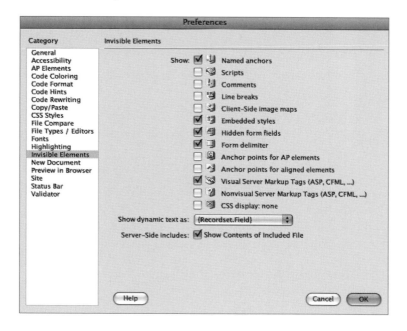

You can see the included file in Design view and in Live view. However, it may not render in a browser while it is still located on your hard drive. The file must be uploaded to a server configured to work with server-side includes to be rendered in a browser.

Now use Dreamweaver to insert an include command into a page.

3 In naxos.html, in the footer, delete the entire <p> that you copied in the previous exercise.

4 Choose Insert > Server-Side Include.

5 In the Select File dialog box, navigate to the lesson10 > includes folder. Select footer.html and click Choose.

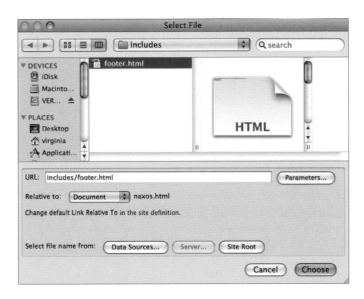

You see the included snippet in the footer in Design view. In the Code view, you see only the include command.

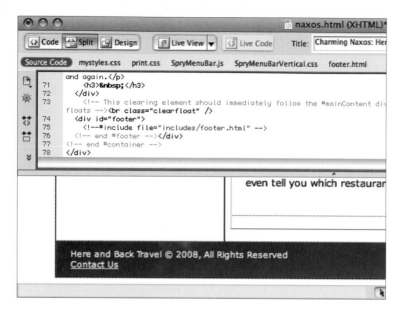

Unlike Library items, the code snippet is not added to the page in Dreamweaver; it is added on the server. All you see in the code in Dreamweaver is the include command.

6 Click the Design button to return to Design view. Select the included text in the Document window.

The Properties panel for SSI (server-side includes) contains an Edit button that allows you to make changes to the included file. You'll work with that in the next exercise.

7 Choose File > Save.

8 Click Live View to see that the included HTML appears right where you want it when the page is rendered. Click Live View again to return to Edit mode.

Adding the server-side include to site pages

To really get the benefit of a server-side include, it needs to be used on every page in the site, instead of the existing footer material. Let's start with about.html.

1 In the Files panel, in the lesson10 folder, double-click about.html to open it.

2 Click anywhere in the footer text.

3 In the tag selector, select the <p> tag. Press Delete.

4 Choose Insert > Server-Side Include.

5 In the Select File dialog box, navigate to the lesson10 > includes folder. Select footer.html and click Choose.

6 Choose File > Save, and then choose File > Close.

Repeat steps 1–6 for the following files: contact.html, form_processing.html, index.html, ourclients.html, santorini.html, and umbria.html.

You've created a server-side include and inserted it on every page in the site.

Updating server-side includes

When you worked with templates and Library items earlier in this lesson, a change to a template or Library item was automatically reproduced on all the pages made from that template. Then each newly updated page was uploaded to the server. When using SSIs, the only file that must be uploaded is the include file.

Let's change the include file and see how Dreamweaver handles the change.

1 In the Files panel, in the lesson10 folder, double-click naxos.html to open it.

2 Select the include text in the footer.

3 In the Properties panel, click Edit.

4 The footer.html file opens. Position your mouse pointer after *Contact Us* and press Shift+Return (Windows) or Shift+Enter (Mac) to create a line break.

5 Type **Telephone: (555) 555-5555** on the new line.

6 Choose File > Save. Close the footer.html file.

7 Open any other page in the site that contains the include file and notice that the footer in that file was changed instantly when you changed the included footer. html file.

You've created a server-side include, added it to several pages, and updated it. Many other web-page elements—such as logos, menus, privacy notices, and banners—can be made into easily maintained server-side includes.

You've learned how to use three Dreamweaver productivity tools—templates, Library items, and server-side includes—that help you build pages and update sites. Although you've acquired these skills near the end of this book, choosing to use them is a decision you should make when first creating a new site. Use these tools during your design and page-building process to speed up your workflow and make maintenance easier.

Review questions

1 How do you create a template from an existing page?

2 Name an essential element in a template. Why is it essential?

3 How do you create a child page from a template?

4 How do you create a Library item?

5 How do you add a Library item to a page?

6 How do you create a server-side include file?

7 How do you add a server-side include to a page?

Review answers

1 Choose File > Save as Template and enter the name of the template in the dialog box.

2 The editable region is essential to working with templates because without it the child pages would be locked and uneditable.

3 Choose File > New, and in the New Document dialog box, select Pages from Templates, locate the desired template, and click Create.

4 Select the content on the page that you want to add to the Library. Choose Modify > Library > Add Object to Library. In the Assets panel Library window, name the Library item.

5 Set an insertion point in the document for the Library item. In the Assets panel, select the Library item and click the Insert button.

6 Open a new, blank HTML document. Enter the content. In Code view, remove any page elements from the code except the content you want included. Save the file.

7 Set an insertion point in the document where you want the included file to appear when the page is rendered on the server. Choose Insert > Server-Side Include. In the Select File dialog box, navigate to the appropriate file and choose it.

11 PUBLISHING TO THE WEB

In this lesson, you'll publish your website to the Internet and do the following:

- Define a remote site
- Put files on the web
- Cloak files and folders
- Get pages from the web

 This lesson will take about 45 minutes to complete. Be sure you have copied Lessons > lesson11 from the *Adobe Dreamweaver CS4 Classroom in a Book* CD to your hard drive before beginning.

Dreamweaver's Files panel works as an FTP application that can put files onto a server and keep a site synchronized.

Defining a remote site

Dreamweaver is based on a two-site system. One site is in a folder on your computer's hard drive and is known as the *local site*. All work in the previous lessons has been performed on your local site. The second site, called the *remote site*, is established in a folder on a web server running on another computer. The remote site is generally connected to the Internet and publicly available.

Dreamweaver supports several methods for connecting to a remote site:

- FTP (File Transfer Protocol)—The standard method for connecting to hosted websites.

- Local/Network—A local or network connection is most frequently used with an intermediate web server, called a *staging server*. Files from the staging server are eventually published to an Internet-connected web server.

- WebDav (Distributed Authoring and Versioning)—A web-based system also known to Windows XP users as Web Folders.

- RDS (Remote Development Services)—Developed by Adobe for ColdFusion and primarily used when working with ColdFusion-based sites.

- Microsoft Visual SourceSafe—A version-control system that features check-in/check-out management and rollback capabilities.

In the next exercises, you'll set up a remote site using the two most common methods: FTP and Local/Network.

Setting up a remote FTP site

The vast majority of Web developers rely on FTP to publish and maintain their sites. FTP is a well-established protocol, and many variations of the protocol are used on the web, most of which are supported by Dreamweaver.

1 Open Adobe Dreamweaver CS4.

2 If necessary, press F8 to open the Files panel.

3 Choose Site > Manage Sites.

4 When the Manage Sites dialog box appears, you will see a list of all the sites that you may have defined. If more than one is displayed, make sure that the current site, DW CIB, is chosen. Choose Edit.

5 In the "Site Definition for DW CIB" dialog box, click the Advanced tab, and from the Category list, select Remote Info.

Note: The following two exercises are mutually exclusive. If you have an Internet host and the details for establishing an FTP connection, follow the steps in "Setting up a remote FTP site." If you have direct access to a web server, follow the steps in "Establishing a remote site on a local or network server."

Note: To perform this exercise, you need access to a remote FTP server, including FTP address, user name, and password.

▶ **Tip:** To directly open the Site Definition for the current site without opening the Manage Site dialog box, double-click DW CIB in the pop-up menu at the top where all defined sites are listed.

6 From the Access pop-up menu, choose FTP.

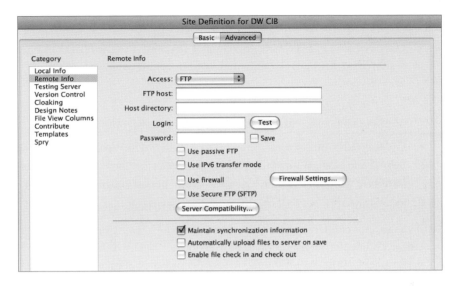

7 In the FTP host field, type the URL of your FTP server.

Typically, an FTP address looks something like this: ftp.mySite.com. If you're unsure of the correct FTP address, contact your web host.

8 In the "Host directory" field, type the name of the folder that contains documents publicly accessible to the web, if any.

Some Web hosts provide FTP access to a root-level folder that might contain non-public folders—such as cgi-bin, which is used to store CGI (Common Gateway Interface) or binary scripts—as well as a public folder. In these cases, type the public folder name—such as *public_html*, *wwwroot*, or *www*—in the "Host directory" field. In other web host configurations, the FTP address is the same as the public folder, and the "Host directory" field should be left blank.

9 In the Login field, type your FTP user name, and in the Password field, type your FTP password. Both fields are frequently case-sensitive, so be sure you type carefully.

10 Click Test to verify that your FTP connection works properly.

11 Dreamweaver displays an alert to notify you if the connection was successful or unsuccessful. Click OK to dismiss the alert.

12 If you don't want to reenter your user name and password every time Dreamweaver connects to your site, select Save. Make sure you have a record of your password elsewhere, because you won't be able to read it as text here.

13 Consult the instructions from your hosting company to select the appropriate options for your specific FTP server. In most cases, Use Secure FTP is a good choice. The options are::

- Use passive FTP—Allows your computer to connect to the host computer and bypass a firewall restraint; often used in conjunction with the "Use firewall" option.

- Use IPv6 transfer mode—Enables connection to IPv6-based servers, which utilize the most recent version of the Internet transfer protocol.

- Use firewall—Allows your computer to connect to the host computer from behind a firewall. When this option is selected, click the Firewall Settings button to define firewall preferences, such as port number and firewall host.

- Use Secure FTP (SFTP)—Enables connection to hosts using SFTP.

14 If you cannot connect to your FTP server, click the Server Compatibility button. When the Server Compatibility dialog box opens, deselect the "Use FTP performance optimization" option, click OK, and click "Test again."

15 Select any desired options for working with your remote site:

- Maintain synchronization information—Automatically notes which files have been changed on the local and remote sites so that they can be easily synchronized. This feature helps you keep track of your changes and can be helpful if you change multiple pages before you upload. You may want to use cloaking with this feature. You'll learn about cloaking in an upcoming exercise.

- Automatically upload files to server on save—Transfers files from the local to remote site when they are saved. This option can become annoying if you save often and aren't yet ready for a page to go public.

- Enable file check in and check out—Starts the Check In/Check Out system for collaborative website building with other team members. If you choose this option, you'll need to enter a user name for check-out purposes and, optionally, an e-mail address. If you're working by yourself, you do not need to select file check in/check out.

It is acceptable to leave all three of these options deselected.

16 Click OK. A dialog box appears informing you that the cache will be recreated because you changed the site settings. Click OK. When Dreamweaver finishes updating the cache, click Done to close the Manage Sites dialog box.

Establishing a remote site on a local or network server

If your company or organization uses a staging server as a "middleman" between web designers and the live website, it's likely that you'll need to connect to your remote site through a local or network server. You can also use this type of connection on your own system, if it includes a web server.

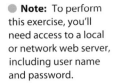 **Note:** To perform this exercise, you'll need access to a local or network web server, including user name and password.

1 Open Adobe Dreamweaver CS4.

2 If necessary, press F8 to open the Files panel.

3 Choose Site > Manage Sites.

4 When the Manage Sites dialog box appears, make sure that the current site, DW CIB, is chosen. Click Edit.

5 In the "Site Definition for DW CIB" dialog box, click the Advanced tab, and choose Remote Info from the Category list.

6 From the Access pop-up menu, choose Local/Network.

▶ **Tip:** To directly open the Site Definition for the current site without opening the Manage Site dialog box, double-click DW CIB in the pop-up menu at the top where all defined sites are listed.

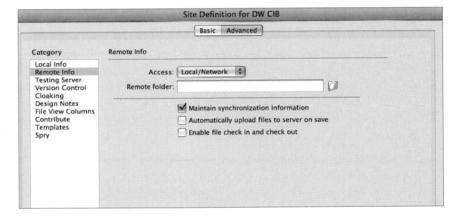

If you're using the web server on your own system as a remote folder, click the folder icon and browse to the folder. The address may be similar to [*system drive*]: \Inetpub\wwwroot (Windows), or [*system drive*]:Users [*user name*]:Sites (Mac). If you are using a network server, navigate to the specific server on your network.

7 Select the appropriate options for working with your remote site:

- Maintain synchronization information—Automatically notes which files have been changed on both the local and remote sites so that they can be easily synchronized. This feature helps you track changes and can be helpful if you change multiple pages before you upload. You may want to use cloaking with this feature. You'll learn about cloaking in an upcoming exercise.

- Automatically upload files to server on save—Transfers files from the local site to the remote site when they are saved. This selection can grow annoying if you save often and aren't yet ready for a page to go public.

- Enable file check in and check out—Starts the Check In/Check Out system for collaborative website building with other team members. If you select this option, you'll need to enter a user name for check-out purposes and, optionally, an e-mail address. If you're working by yourself, you do not need to select file check in/check out.

It is acceptable to leave all three of these options deselected.

8 Click OK.

Cloaking folders and files

Note: Cloaked folders and files are transferred when you Put an entire site or when the Put Dependant Files option is used. Later, they can be deleted manually from the remote site.

If you selected "Maintain synchronization information" for a remote site using FTP or a network server, you may want to *cloak* some of the local materials. All the files in your site root may not need to be transferred to the remote server. There's no point in filling remote storage space with files that won't be accessed or will remain inaccessible to the website user. For example, Template and Library folders don't need to be transferred to the remote server. Some Photoshop (.psd), Flash (.fla), or other files used to create your site may not need to be on the remote server. You can cloak items so that Dreamweaver will not synchronize those local site items with items on the remote site. Folders, file types, and individual files that are cloaked are excluded from the synchronization process.

Start by setting up cloaking in the Site Definitions.

1 If necessary, press F8 to open the Files panel, and choose DW CIB from the site list.

2 Choose Site > Manage Sites.

3 When the Manage Sites dialog box appears, make sure that the current site, DW CIB, is chosen, and click Edit.

4 In the Cloaking category, select "Enable cloaking" and "Cloak files ending with." Click OK. Dreamweaver may update the cache. If so, after the cache is updated, click Done to close the "Site Definition for DW CIB" dialog box.

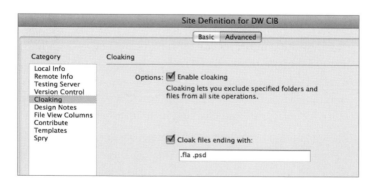

Dreamweaver suggests cloaking files with .fla and .psd extensions. You can add file extensions to the "Cloak files ending with" field if you have other file types, such as Adobe Illustrator (.ai), that you want to cloak. Cloaked files are indicated by a red slash in the Files panel.

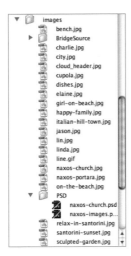

You can also cloak specific files or folders.

5   From the Files list, select the Library folder.

6   Right-click (Windows) or Control-click (Mac) the selected folder and choose Cloaking > Cloak. A dialog box appears warning that "Cloaking template or library files will only affect put or get commands, not any batch site operation." Click OK.

7   In the Files list, expand the SpryAssets folder. Select SpryAccordion-finished.css.

8   Right-click (Windows) or Control-click (Mac) the selected folder and choose Cloaking > Cloak from the menu.

Using the Site Definitions dialog box and the Cloaking context menu, you cloaked file types, folders, and files. The synchronization process ignores those cloaked items.

Putting your site online

For the most part, the local site and the remote site are mirror images, containing the same HTML files, images, and assets in identical folder structures. When you transfer a web page from your local site to your remote site, you are publishing, or *putting*, that page. If you *put* a file stored in a folder in your local site, Dreamweaver transfers the file to the equivalent folder on the remote site. It will even automatically create the remote folder, if necessary.

Using Dreamweaver, you can publish anything from a single file to a complete site in a single operation. When you publish a web page, Dreamweaver asks if you would also like to put the dependent files. Dependent files are the images, Flash movies, JavaScript files, CSS external style sheets, server-side includes, and all other files necessary to complete the page. Dreamweaver automatically puts all of your dependent files in the proper remote folders to match their locations on your local site.

● **Note:** This exercise assumes that you have established a remote site, using either an FTP or local/network connection as described earlier in this lesson.

1   In the Files panel, expand the lesson11 folder.

2   Click the "Connects to remote host" button 🔌 to connect to the remote site.

3   Select test-page.html.

4   On the Document toolbar, click the File Management menu button 🔼 , to choose Put File(s).

You can choose Site > Put for the current page, or select the file in the Files panel and choose Put File(s) (the up arrow button). You can also use the Files panel to transfer multiple files. Select the content you want to transfer—individual files or complete folders—and click the Put Files button.

● **Note:** The first time you upload, it's generally helpful to include dependent files. If you do so, everything related to a page—images, SpryAssets, CSS files, scripts, and .swf files—is uploaded automatically. However, you might not want to upload dependent files if you've just changed the code on the page and have not altered any of the associated images or other attached assets.

5   When the Dependent Files dialog box appears, click Yes. If you don't click anything, the Dependent Files dialog box will choose "No" by default and dismiss itself.

6   To see what is on the remote server, from the menu at the upper right of the Files panel, choose Remote view.

✓	Local view
	Remote view
	Testing server
	Repository view

7   To display local and remote files in a side-by-side display, click "Expand to show local and remote sites" 🗗 , the last button to the right of the Files panel.

Dreamweaver re-creates your local site structure on the remote site. You should see a lesson11 folder and an images folder. The test-page.html file should be in the lesson11 folder. The bench.jpg file should be in the images folder.

● **Note:** Dreamweaver transfers files as a separate computer process, so you can continue working while the files are published.

The opposite of Put is *Get*. You can *get* any file from the remote site by selecting it in the Remote or Local pane and clicking Get (the down arrow). Alternatively, you can drag the file from the remote site pane to the local site pane. It is important to note that a file transferred from one site to another automatically overwrites the file on a destination site.

8 When you're done exploring, click "Disconnect from remote host" to break the connection.

9 Use a browser to connect to the remote site on the Internet or on your network server. Type the exact URL in the browser location bar, including folders and filename on the remote site (for example, www.yourserver.com/lesson11/test-page.html). You should see the test page in the browser, with both text and image displayed.

Testing the file transfer. The image should transfer as a dependent file.

In this lesson, you set up your Site Definition to connect to a remote server and uploaded files to that remote site. You also cloaked files and folders.

You're now ready to set up a connection to your own website and use Dreamweaver's file-transfer options to move your websites from your computer onto the World Wide Web. You have finished all the exercises and are ready to plan, create, and publish a site of your own. Congratulations!

Review questions

1 What is a remote site?

2 Name two types of file transfer supported in Dreamweaver.

3 How can you configure Dreamweaver so that it does not synchronize certain files in your site root folder with the server?

4 True or false? You have to manually publish every file and associated image, JavaScript file, and server-side include.

Review answers

1 A remote site is a mirror image of your local site; the remote site is stored on a web server connected to the Internet.

2 FTP (File Transfer Protocol) and Local/Network are the two most commonly used file transfer methods. Other file-transfer methods supported in Dreamweaver include WebDav, Visual SourceSafe, and RDS.

3 Cloak the files or folders for which you do not want to maintain synchronization.

4 False. Dreamweaver will automatically transfer dependent files, if desired, including embedded or referenced images, CSS style sheets, and Flash movies.

INDEX

The fastest, easiest, most comprehensive way to learn Adobe® Creative Suite® 4

Classroom in a Book®, the best-selling series of hands-on software training books, helps you learn the features of Adobe software quickly and easily.

The **Classroom in a Book** series offers what no other book or training program does—an official training series from Adobe Systems, developed with the support of Adobe product experts.

To see a complete list of our Adobe® Creative Suite® 4 titles go to www.peachpit.com/adobecs4

Adobe**Press**